110379

A Programme for Full Employment in the 1990s

Report of the Kreisky Commission on Employment Issues in Europe

Pergamon Titles of Related Interest

GIARINI
Cycles, Value & Employment: Responses to the Economic Crisis

GIARINI
The Emerging Service Economy

KERR
The Common Market & How It Works, 3rd edition

Pergamon Journals of Related Interest

Contemporary European Affairs

Socio-Economic Planning Sciences

Technology in Society

World Development

TLDP : TLD MB [M]
1989

A Programme for Full Employment in the 1990s

Report of the Kreisky Commission on Employment Issues in Europe

COMMISSION ON
EMPLOYMENT ISSUES IN EUROPE

PERGAMON PRESS

OXFORD · NEW YORK · BEIJING · FRANKFURT
SÃO PAULO · SYDNEY · TOKYO · TORONTO

U.K.	Pergamon Press plc, Headington Hill Hall, Oxford OX3 0BW, England
U.S.A.	Pergamon Press, Inc., Maxwell House, Fairview Park, Elmsford, New York 10523, U.S.A.
PEOPLE'S REPUBLIC OF CHINA	Pergamon Press, Room 4037, Qianmen Hotel, Beijing, People's Republic of China
FEDERAL REPUBLIC OF GERMANY	Pergamon Press GmbH, Hammerweg 6, D-6242 Kronberg, Federal Republic of Germany
BRAZIL	Pergamon Editora Ltda, Rua Eça de Queiros, 346, CEP 04011, Paraiso, São Paulo, Brazil
AUSTRALIA	Pergamon Press Australia Pty Ltd., P.O. Box 544, Potts Point, N.S.W. 2011, Australia
JAPAN	Pergamon Press, 5th Floor, Matsuoka Central Building, 1-7-1 Nishishinjuku, Shinjuku-ku, Tokyo 160, Japan
CANADA	Pergamon Press Canada Ltd., Suite No. 271, 253 College Street, Toronto, Ontario, Canada M5T 1R5

First edition 1989

Library of Congress Cataloging-in-Publication Data

Commission on Employment Issues in Europe.
A programme for full employment in the 1990's: report of the Kreisky Commission on Employment Issues in Europe/Commission on Employment Issues in Europe.
— 1st ed.
p. cm
Bibliography: p.
1. Manpower policy — Europe. 2. Unemployment — Europe. I. Title.
dc19 89-3825
HD5764.A6C664 1989 339.5'094 —

British Library Cataloguing in Publication Data

Commission on Employment Issues in Europe
A programme for full employment in the 1990s: report of the Kreisky Commission on Employment Issues in Europe
1. Europe. Employment
I. Title
331.1'25'094
ISBN 0-08-037761-0 Hardcover
ISBN 0-08-037760-2 Flexicover

Printed in Great Britain by BPCC Wheatons Ltd, Exeter

Contents

List of Figures and Tables

Introduction

BRUNO KREISKY

WHEN I was asked to set up a commission with the purpose of tackling the problem of unemployment in Europe, my initial response was: it would have to be a commission that would not be made up entirely of economists. The problem would have to be analyzed from various angles and therefore called for a diversity of participants. In addition, I had worries about myself. I am an old man, having arrived at an age at which one does not easily start something new—and this was a new task.

A number of good friends, Professor Galbraith among others, advised me to accept this important task nevertheless. John Galbraith used the following words. "I very much applaud the enterprise. The stubborn persistence of unemployment is one of the great problems of all the industrialized countries. The problem has to be examined in the context of relevant solutions, and there is nobody better qualified to do so than you."

George Ball said: "The project you describe appears to me to be of extraordinary importance. Of course I am in favour of you as the chairman of the commission. You should not let your age deter you from doing this."

Professor Biedenkopf supported the project by stating that "it is essential to deal with the subject because the danger of a further increase in unemployment is not discussed sufficiently or at all at present".

James Callaghan wrote: "I would like to encourage you to do everything you can to see that the commission is established."

And Michel Rocard replied that he would like to be present at the constituent meeting of the commission.

I wish to express my thanks to Professor Galbraith, George Ball, Professor Biedenkopf, James Callaghan and Michel Rocard—who I mention as representing many others—for having encouraged me to accept this difficult task.

Please allow me to briefly expound on my long-standing, close association with Professor Galbraith, whom I met in 1953. I have been in contact with him ever since and now, after 35 years, I must say that I hold him in high esteem, not only as a brilliant scientist but also as a remarkable person and human being.

I am very glad that, in spite of my serious illness, there has been no significant delay in compiling the commission's report and that I am now able to present the results. I would also like to explain why I made a special effort to attend the meetings of the commission as often as possible, despite the difficulties. A number of people seem to think that I was primarily concerned with foreign affairs during my long political career. That is not the case and calls for some clarification.

The various features and problems of the labour market have been a long-standing and foremost concern of mine. My experience of the terrible Great Depression of the 1930s had a profound effect on all my activities from the start, and I firmly believe in a causal link between the world economic crisis and the subsequent downfall of European democracies. The Second World War, up to now the world's greatest political catastrophe, was largely brought about by economic pressures. This fact needs to be emphasized, as a misreading of history could easily lead to a strictly political interpretation of what happened.

While I was primarily concerned with the problem of unemployment in the course of my political career, I was also preoccupied with the problem of peace. Although I was aware that there were limitations on what could be done, I perceived a restricted but none the less important task for Austria.

I find it hard to believe that the economic cycle alone was responsible for overcoming the Great Depression. I am convinced that preparations for the war and the ensuing war itself resolved the problem of large-scale unemployment. The peacetime economy would not have been able to accomplish this.

When during the Second World War, Beveridge demanded full employment and also established corresponding criteria, this seemed to me one of the most important lessons to be learned from contemporary political experience. To my great disappointment, leading economists have abandoned the principle of full employment in recent years. I have never done so. It represents a definition of one's position, which I could not abandon.

Of course the whole issue of full employment has now to be viewed from a different angle, its psychological meaning being different. Yet there are specific symptoms that have to be recognized at an early stage, if we are not to be confronted by problems that before long would pose a threat to our democratic security. I would like to illustrate this by citing a recent experience. I was watching a TV broadcast of a soccer game that featured an English and an Italian team. As the sports commentators were apparently interested in the expected riots, the TV cameras focused on certain details. One such detail, which impressed me very much, showed a number of British youngsters, all of whom were holding up swastikas and asking: "Do you know what this is? Why does it bother you so much?"

This incident may of course appear of minor concern but someone of my generation and our experiences cannot possibly ignore it. There has, in fact, been a significant destabilization in Western Europe. I recall the considerable nervousness over the recent French elections. However, France is only one of several countries in which such manifestations have been observed.

By now it will be obvious to the reader that I see many of the issues discussed here within a political context. The great economic crisis led to a very significant historical event, namely the Second World War. This should be a warning to us. The immense human sacrifices caused by this war have to be seen in this light. Our view of the various historical aspects has to be sharpened.

Only recently has there been a change towards a better understanding between nations and there is hope that efforts on the part of the world powers to prevent war will be successful. During the past few months, efforts have been made to achieve greater security in Europe, justifiably giving rise to optimism. Issues concerning world economic development are thus gaining additional importance. European integration and East–West economic relations are of renewed interest. Although I am aware of the difficulties that will be encountered along the way, I believe Europe will fulfil the preconditions for her further development. Some of these preconditions are already recognizable.

During the last few years, fighting unemployment has found relatively little political support. A kind of depoliticization of the problem appears to have taken place. I consider this a misguided attitude which could have disastrous consequences. I cannot cease to warn of the effect of long-term unemployment and its social implications in democratic European countries. The impression that we are dealing with an unsolvable problem of employment in the democratic parts of Europe is misleading. It could easily induce politicians to give lesser priority to the problem of unemployment, paying only lip service to it.

To date only a very few countries have taken sweeping measures to fight unemployment. Since 1973 many countries have adopted policies with different priorities, with security within society given lower ranking. We have reason to take a renewed interest in these issues and not to give way to a fatalistic view of developments. The fact that opinions vary greatly on this subject poses a challenge which, in turn, is almost a necessity.

I have dealt with this particular task in great depth, for example, at the Socialist International which, so to speak, is based on a system of division of labour. Willy Brandt, as is generally known, devoted himself to the recommendations made by his North–South commission. It must be stressed that the theoretical findings of this commission are truly sensational. Putting the individual proposals into practice has proved to be more difficult. Nonetheless, it must be said: there is hardly an issue nowadays in this field that has not at some point been subject to contemplation by Willy Brandt's commission.

Olof Palme concerned himself primarily with the problem of security and disarmament. Gro Harlem Brundtland and her Commission recently analyzed ecological problems in a very comprehensive manner.

While at the Socialist International, I was chiefly concerned with issues regarding the Middle East and employment policies.

A few of us were appointed to office and had a chance to put our ideas and experience into practice. The events of my youth having made a lasting impression on me, I, as a politician in office, consistently attempted to keep in mind the experiences of the Great Depression. Already in 1972, on the occasion of the party conference in Villach, I drew attention to the danger of unemployment.

Nevertheless, it should be mentioned that for many years Austria was among the few countries in the world to which the maxim of full employment could be applied. This greatly contributed towards our prestige in the world. The American economist and Nobel laureate Wassily Leontieff, among others, thus spoke of an "Austrian way". We would have been poor political strategists had we not capitalized on this catchphrase, as coined by such a prominent economist. The question as to whether our political course could be termed "Austro-Keynesianism", without underestimating Keynes, would seem futile.

Quite early in my political career I was intent on preventing an economic crisis. I still recall an evening, in the course of which one of my ministers exclaimed: "I can't understand why Chancellor Kreisky's constantly referring to a crisis.'' This was early in 1975, when I was advocating the prevention of a major crisis, while the economists were talking about stabilization.

What then, to me, appears to be of significance in the current situation, without my endorsing a superficial historicism? I will gladly leave all purely economic issues to the experts of the commission. I believe, however, that we are currently experiencing a ''twilight of the gods'' in modern economics. So-called theoretical axioms—such as monetarism—which developed out of the controversy between doctrines, in time are destined to become meaningless.

I would like to single out just a few points of the report which, to me, are of particular importance and where I detect additional potential for employment:

Environmental protection. This concept will play a dominant role in politics in the coming years. Although environmental protection will be costly, it will be of great significance in relation to the quality of life. Large sums will have to be set aside within national budgets, adding up to at least the amount currently being used for defence expenditure. But seeing that people are prepared to provide governments with enormous sums of money for armaments, why shouldn't they be willing to do the same for the purpose of saving the environment?

Irrespective of how the problem of environmental protection will eventually be solved, it will serve to create an unforeseeable number of jobs—including jobs of a traditional type, such as those dealing with filtering systems and waste disposal.

At a conference not long ago, some of the more

traditional economists still claimed that environmental protection would not have any effect on the labour market situation. Today we know better than that.

To decry these contemplations as farfetched would be tantamount to disastrous shortsightedness. It was the destiny of so many of us to be labelled visionaries and hopeless idealists until this "twilight of the gods" occurred. What seemed like a vision to us some time ago, today is an irrefutable necessity. Take, for example, warnings about the shrinking ozone layer that surrounds the earth, now an issue of pressing concern.

Our imagination is restrained, in the sense that we are easily led to believe that we have run up against economic bounds. In fact we are often the victims of our limited imagination. Once again I feel obliged to quote Albert Einstein: "Imagination is more important than knowledge."

Infrastructure. In the light of overall European development—and one will increasingly have to think in those terms—the backlog demand for infrastructure investment is very considerable. It is sufficient to refer to the potential inherent in European integration; this potential appears even greater if one thinks in continental terms.

Culture and education. At present we are faced with a high rate of unemployment among well-qualified people: teachers, medical doctors, those involved in cultural activities. The problem may be greater in political terms than numerically. There is a widely accepted notion that if a blue collar worker becomes unemployed, this is an inescapable destiny. Those working in the cultural field are affected by unemployment in a different way. To them unemployment is something to be challenged so that, in turn, public opinion is influenced.

Tackling this particular problem could also be significant in combatting shortcomings in the quality of life which affect large parts of the civilized world.

Development aid. There can be no doubt that development aid will have to be dealt with in a different way than in the past. Constructive individuals can no longer ignore the fact that development aid has been a *de facto* failure in large parts of the world. One example, as proof, is the fiasco of international debt policies.

I sincerely hope that these new aid concepts, which are consistent with a realistic view of things, will come to the fore. I once spoke of a "Marshall Plan" for the developing countries. We must give the developing countries better assistance in their endeavour to establish infrastructure. Ideally, help would be extended to a country such that it was enabled to continue development itself. Instead, many manufacturing plants in developing countries turned into "ghost factories", simply because the native population did not know what to do with them.

I hope we will succeed in drawing people's attention to the meaning and danger of unemployment in modern industrialized countries. We do not wish to present new interpretations of the problem of unemployment but, instead, to offer suggestions for a solution to the problem. There are a number of major problems which we will have to deal with in the coming years, in ways that will have considerable potential for employment.

I firmly believe that the issue of unemployment is of crucial importance to our development. Very soon we shall see that the nonchalance customary nowadays could have grave consequences and could lead to a serious destabilization of European politics.

One does not become aware of the critical nature of the political situation all of a sudden, but gradually through various manifestations. Having to put up with a basically disastrous situation gives rise to indifference on the part of the general population and this could become a serious threat to democracy. The resigned acceptance of a "two-thirds society", which can be observed throughout large parts of Europe, not only bears a danger of depoliticization but also one of hopelessness at not being able to change things for the better.

We are gradually being confronted with a new form of impoverishment, a new type of pauperization. It could hardly be the intention of a progressive democracy to allow this sort of thing to happen. We could easily lose sight of the sociopolitical consequences of such a situation. The dreadful development in regard to narcotics and related crime should be ample warning to us. It may well be that within certain political circles, the opinion holds sway that this is merely a problem of crime and law enforcement. Anyone who succumbs to this deception should not be surprised if the dangers soon attain vast proportions.

It is high time that we realized that geographical demarcations, particularly of environmental policies in certain parts of Europe, are becoming more and more pointless—especially if it is hoped thereby to create geopolitical (I have deliberately chosen this term) delimitations.

The fact is, we know how "continental" the problems of environmental protection are and we know very well just how dramatic the situation has become in terms of climate. What conclusions can be drawn for the development of Western Europe and of Eastern Europe? If we are boldly to go about remedying even short-term problems, we will most urgently have to adopt a different approach to foreign policy.

How much time do we have left to prevent final disasters from occurring? I am convinced that we will soon be confronted with these dangers on a worldwide scale or, at minimum, at a European level.

Here we will have to aim at solutions that should also apply extensively to employment policies. Vast reserves of labour could be put to use? It will depend on our courage whether we will be able to come up with the required large-scale innovative solutions. I just wish to point to these issues, the Commission having dealt with them in depth.

Perhaps this report will be criticized for not having come up with something dramatically new. The temptation to make this criticism is always great, as it is with reproaches concerning the absence of pragmatic political views. Nevertheless, I believe we have highlighted certain issues which should have new topical relevance. This will become very evident in the light of developments in the Soviet Union, the United States and Europe. I would welcome the possibility of various of our arguments becoming audible. I would like to call to mind a statement made by Bertrand Russell: "At times, moral ideas go hand in hand with political developments. Sometimes, however, they are far ahead of the latter."

Suggestions for solutions to unemployment can be traced back to the beginnings of the world economic crisis in the 1930s. Nowadays they do not seem as imaginative as they did then. I would like to cite an example that, being characterized by simplicity as well as a wealth of ideas, has to be regarded as a lost opportunity. In 1931 the great Austrian politician and Social Democrat Otto Bauer made a then sensational as well as "unrealistic" proposal which even today remains fascinating. He suggested an international public loan for the benefit of Central Europe, stating:

> "Vast capital is not being utilized to advantage in the United States of America, in France and in the neutral European countries and, while it is not being used, the national economy of Central Europe is desperately in need of such capital. Undoubtedly one of the most effective methods of controlling the world crisis and unemployment would be to redirect this capital into production, thereby reviving the latter."

The countries that could benefit from such a "Marshall Plan" are, of course, different today: namely, the Eastern European, African and Asian countries, with varying degrees of priority.

Generally, people associate the issue of unemployment primarily with a lack of income. However, in the modern welfare state this issue alone is not decisive. I continue to be impressed by a statement that Professor Biedenkopf made during one of our meetings, when he remarked that the problem of unemployment did not play a very important part in the current German election campaign. The victory of neoconservatism has been, in this respect, also a psychological phenomenon. If I may say so, to me as a Social Democrat, it appears that those who should have done away with unemployment lost faith early on. Only a very few remained true to themselves, refusing prematurely and rashly to give up principles which had been established decades ago and were still of relevance. Among the few, one man stood out like a lighthouse: J. K. Galbraith. But currently the number of those who are not prepared indiscriminately to accept the ruling pseudo-doctrines is increasing.

Perhaps the problem of unemployment has not played a decisive role in Europe during recent elections. However, this will not necessarily remain the case, considering that history is measured in terms of decades while politics is measured in terms of legislative periods.

All those who feel that the ideas expressed here are not in keeping with public opinion should be reminded that in West Germany a recently conducted opinion poll revealed that nearly 60 per cent of those questioned were in favour of cyclically higher tax returns being spent on job-creation schemes.

In the course of the commission's work, there were some fascinating discussions, for example, about the "working poor". This appropriate term was coined in the United States and refers to those individuals who have work but are barely able to make a living. With millions of people affected, this calls for a revolutionary change of thinking. Of the reliable supporters of trade unionism, as we have known it since the beginnings of industrialization, many are nowadays employed in declining occupations. One just has to think of the labour aristocracy of the graphic arts and the metal industry. In order to prevent anarchical developments, workers in precarious jobs will soon need to be won over to unionism if we are not to be helplessly confronted with unexpected "explosions".

As can be observed, even social problems that have developed more recently could be remedied by means of seemingly older methods. This brings to mind a minor episode. Shortly after the First World War, when dismayed civil servants complained about their situation to Otto Bauer, who had then become the new Undersecretary of State for Foreign Affairs, he said to them: "Gentlemen, you will simply have to organize." Some time afterwards several colleagues still related this conversation somewhat appalled. Today, government officials represent the best organized union in Austria.

Apart from a number of experiences which I am currently putting in writing, this publication will probably be my last one to be presented to the public. Once again I have come to the realization that we are still not living in the best of all possible worlds—in spite of assurances by the various apologists. There are still great tasks ahead. One can only hope they will be accomplished, but one cannot expect it with certainty.

I felt myself to be an objective chairman of the commission, in the sense of being an objective, open-minded listener. I was not always prepared to support what my fellow speakers had to say. Thus participation at meetings of this commission did not entail an obligation to be wholly in agreement with the final report.

Lastly, a quotation by the Catholic writer Georges Bernanos served as my guide-line:

> "Je suis ici pour dire la verité. Un homme dit la verité quand il dit ce qu'il pense. Dire ce qu'on pense c'est donner toute la part de verité dont on dispose et le Bon Dieu meme n'en demande pas plus." (I am here to tell the truth. A man tells the truth when he tells what he thinks. To tell what one thinks, that means to give the whole part of the truth that one disposes of. Even God does not ask for more.)

I know it proved somewhat of a surprise to the members of the commission that I took my task as chairman so seriously, also making an effort to structure the content of the work of the commission. That applies equally to this report, for which I feel a great sense of personal responsibility.

I wish to thank my close co-workers in the commission, Clas-Erik Odhner, David Lea, Paavo Lipponen and Mathias Hinterscheid among others, as well as Fritz Klocker, the organizer of our meetings. In particular, I wish to thank my closest co-worker, Ewald Walterskirchen: without him this report would not have appeared.

Recommendations

1. The most important message from the Kreisky Commission is that it is indeed possible to overcome the unemployment crisis in Europe if governments and social partners show the will to co-operate. European governments should coordinate their economic policies to ensure that annual economic growth rates of $3\frac{1}{2}$ per cent—4 per cent a year are sustained. This would allow employment to expand by about $1\frac{1}{2}$ per cent per year and unemployment to fall by 1 percentage point per year. These developments are essential for the success of the single European market strategy. The strongest argument for higher growth, however, is not the generation of employment as such, but the need to meet the enormous demands of our time.

2. Growth must be "qualitative" as well as quantitative. Economic growth can and should be "twisted" so as not to damage but to improve the environment and to provide a higher quality of life and more skilled jobs. Our views are entirely in line with the Brundtland Commission, which also concluded that growth is vital to create the resources necessary to save environment. To "twist" economic growth in this way:

(a)   The protection and improvement of the environment should be an important part of national and

1

European programmes for employment creation.

(b) Technical R & D should increasingly be directed towards finding less polluting and destructive production and consumption methods, and governments should co-operate to ensure their application.

(c) Education should be radically improved for disadvantaged children and young people to encourage them not to drop out of school or resist further training, thereby reducing the problem of "unemployability".

3. Governments are right to be cautious over general demand stimulation to promote growth—but not to the point of paralysis. Growth can be supported and stimulated without incurring undue risks of inflation if more selective and adjustment-promoting policies are adopted on both the demand and the supply side.

(a) In the recent past, a large part of inflation was initially caused by rising commodity prices. Western European governments should now initiate and foster co-operation with other governments worldwide to establish more efficient commodity production and price stabilization schemes.

(b) All countries need to develop efficient labour market policies to help increase employment and to mitigate wage and price pressure at higher levels of employment.

(c) Government and the two sides of industry should develop policies to promote real wage growth through increased productivity rather than high nominal wage increases which are eroded through inflation.

4. Selective policies and programmes must take account of Europe's vast regional diversity. Programmes and supportive measures should be designed both to create employment in disadvantaged regions and to increase geographical mobility. A precondition for development in these regions is the creation of much better infrastructure, though different methods have to be applied to old "smoke-stack" areas and to those peripheral regions where industrialization has never really taken hold. In the former, growth centres can be established and relied upon to spread positive effects. In the latter, improved education and industrial training will be particularly important.

A Six-Point Programme for Growth and Employment

5. These points are reflected in the following programme:

(a) European governments must together develop the infrastructure necessary to reap the fruits of their endeavours to create a free internal market by 1992 and beyond. Key areas for such investments should be telecommunications, rail and road transport, urban renewal and housing.

(b) A new and co-operative approach to environmental protection and improvement is urgently needed now if accumulated damage is not to become irreparable. Expenditure on the environment needs to be at least doubled. A substantial broadening of environmental R & D efforts is also required and international agreements are necessary to prevent environmental "dumping". There must be closer East-West co-operation in Europe; pollution does not respect national frontiers.

(c) Europe's research, technological and innovative programmes should be further strengthened, not only to manage structural change and to ensure competitiveness, but also to improve living standards, working conditions and the quality of life generally. There is scope to build in a greater role for human skills in new technology.

(d) Cultural and educational programmes should be expanded—for their own sake, and also because they can stimulate open-mindedness, experimentation and inventiveness, all of which are increasingly essential in economies now characterized more by "brain" than by "muscle-power" tasks. Unsatisfied demands for cultural services are especially great outside the big cities.

(e) The rapidly growing demand for intermediate information services to other producers (such as software, databanks and consulting, all of which require very good telecommunications links and services) must be met.

(f) The new opportunities that *glasnost* and *perestroika* are creating for more East-West trade and co-operation should be taken up, and Europe's relations with developing countries must be further strengthened.

The Means

6.   Such programmes of course need financing: the rule should be "as much private finance as possible and as much

public finance as necessary''. New jobs must be created and the long-term unemployed must be trained accordingly.

Room for manoeuvre in fiscal policy should not be used for income tax cuts, but for financing long-term economic programmes, since this is a much more efficient and less inflationary strategy. More room for manoeuvre in fiscal policy can be created through enhanced governmental co-ordination. These programmes should not, at least in the initial stage, require a monetary expansion since there is no shortage of funds in capital markets. However, lower interest rates must be sought, both to help economic development and to relieve part of the debt burden of developing countries. Multiplier effects will roughly double the employment created by the intial programmes.

7. Growth policies and programmes must be supported by much stronger labour market policies than presently applied in most countries. A key objective must be to make it possible for young people and the long-term unemployed to secure the training and other help necessary for them to obtain jobs. An active labour market policy should be used to promote employment in non-inflationary ways. Such measures should be concentrated on areas and groups with high unemployment. The costs of increasing production and employment should be reduced by providing training and mobility allowances. But labour market policy is not just for the unemployed: an efficient labour exchange and comprehensive training programmes are indispensable to increase adaptability and smooth structural development by matching job applicants to job vacancies. Improving the operation of labour markets has therefore the additional and considerable benefit of reducing inflationary

pressure.

8. A reduction of working time that takes into account international competitiveness can help to increase employment. Increased labour market flexibility is also required—though this should be "mutual flexibility" with employers as well as workers accepting new working practices.

9. Even if unemployment fell by one percentage point a year, it would still leave unacceptably high levels of unemployment for a number of years. This reinforces the need to establish minimum standards of income for all, for the "working poor" who hold insecure, low-paid jobs, as well as for those on the dole.

Part I: Unemployment in Europe and its Dangers

1. Introduction

> "High unemployment is not really an economic problem, it is a political problem." (Clas-Erik Odhner, at the first Vienna meeting of the Commission)

Something can and must be done to end mass unemployment in Europe, now afflicting nearly 20 million people. That is the central message of this report. We have been concerned to confront the prevailing mood of political defeatism and social apathy towards the problem of unemployment; to show why high levels of joblessness damage not simply the well-being of unemployed people and their families but the economic and social fabric of Western European societies; and to point the way towards a new strategy for tackling unemployment which we believe represents a solid policy foundation on which European governments of all political complexions can build.

The strategy entails a significant acceleration of long-run "qualitative" economic growth, co-ordinated on a

European scale, and brought about by measures which "twist" the nature of economic growth in such a way as to minimize environmental damage and maximize the generation of high-quality jobs, including jobs for those largely bypassed by market forces. The strategy has as its broader aim the enhancement of the quality of life for all Europe's citizens, through opportunities for satisfying employment, a better environment and cultural enrichment.

It is a theme of this report that higher growth is a necessary but insufficient condition to bring unemployment down. Left to itself the market tends to produce and reinforce inequalities—between those in and out of work, between strong and disadvantaged groups in the labour market, between regions and countries. Thus even rapid economic growth may leave many unemployed people untouched. Particularly vulnerable are the unskilled, older workers and minorities, especially in depressed regions.

Our six-point economic programme for Europe aims to boost growth in ways that will spread its benefits widely and contribute to the quality of life. As vital complements to the programme, we advocate labour market policies which break down obstacles to expansion by raising skill levels and increasing adaptability.

The task is all the more urgent in view of steps taken by the governments in the European Community to create a barrier-free common market by the end of 1992. The European Commission itself says that more expansionary policies are essential to reap the full benefits of market integration and to maximize its job-creating effect. A modest stimulus to growth on a co-ordinated basis could more than double the generation of employment by the programme, from 2 to 5 million jobs. This compares with 16 million or so currently out of work in the Community.

The initial impetus for our work arose out of concern that unemployment was increasingly regarded as an intractable problem which, for lack of obvious remedies, was sinking ever lower in the scale of political priorities. A number of Western European governments have abandoned any commitment to full employment. Some have claimed that government cannot determine employment and unemployment levels in the medium and longer term, and that unemployment reflects overly-rigid labour market structures. Others have faced severe constraints in their attempts to tackle unemployment on a national level.

Experience over the past few years has demonstrated that elections can be won by governments presiding over high and even rising unemployment, while opinion polls display a curious insensitivity on the part of many people to the fact that at least a tenth of Europe's workforce is unemployed. These people tend to see unemployment as a social rather than an economic problem, to be mitigated by welfare benefits rather than by measures to create jobs. All these factors have weakened the determination of European political parties across the right-left spectrum to make employment a central policy priority.

The current situation is however inherently unstable. Unemployment blights the lives not only of those directly affected, but of all those who fear that they or their children may become unemployed, or whose job and career prospects are impaired in an economy running below capacity. Nor, we believe, will Europeans indefinitely accept a situation in which perhaps one-third of

PFE—C

society is denied the citizenship rights of income and employment security that others now take for granted.

Work is also more than just a means of securing a livelihood. Sigmund Freud claimed that work is a person's strongest tie with reality. Unemployment means a loss not just of income but of self-confidence and social integration. The erosion of community ties, allied with poverty and feelings of alienation from "normal" life, feed vandalism, violence, even riots. In the long run mass unemployment may pose a real threat to democracy. The world economic crisis of the 1930s which was partly responsible for the rise of fascism stands out as a warning. The strong showing of the extreme right in some recent European elections suggests the parallels are by no means fanciful.

2. Unemployment and precarious jobs

> "Unemployment did not play a decisive role in recent elections." (Kurt Biedenkopf, at the first Vienna meeting of the Commission)

Unemployment in Western Europe has more than quadrupled since 1970, doubling between 1980 and 1988. In many countries unemployment has become chronically high, rising even in "economic upturns". The present one, although stronger, has made very little dent in unemployment so far. Without apparent irony, the OECD wrote in 1985 of the United Kingdom that the "unemployment rate has risen by 2.5 percentage points during the current recovery".[1] In the era of postwar social consensus when governments were committed to full employment policies, such a contradiction in terms would have been unimaginable.

Open unemployment, as reflected in official statistics, is not the whole problem. The nature of employment has changed in ways that have made open unemployment almost certainly a misleading indicator of labour surplus. Workers too discouraged to look for jobs, visible under-employment of those in work, "make-work" jobs under government employment schemes and involuntary part-time work are all signs of pervasive "labour slack".

In the 1980s, increased unemployment has come about mainly through a lengthening of the duration of unemployment. The number of chronic unemployed, out of work for over a year, is more than the total number of jobless in any year of the 1970s. The number of workers joining the dole queues has remained fairly constant in recent years.[2] This is important for policy-making since it implies that efforts should be directed less towards the prevention of lay-offs, which could inhibit necessary structural adjustments, and more towards bringing those unemployed back to work.

Besides the unemployed, large numbers of workers are in precarious jobs with little employment or income security, access to benefits or employment rights.

This fragmentation of the labour market into a majority with secure, well-paid jobs and a minority in various kinds of insecure, often low-paid work has been intensified by government policy and company practice introduced in a climate of sluggish demand for labour. People with low skills are pushed down the job hierarchy, into more and more precarious jobs, or out of work altogether.

Young people, women, older workers and minorities have been the principal victims of "labour slack". In particular, older workers with obsolete skills have been increasingly marginalized in many Western European countries. The extent of their marginalization is often understated by official unemployment rates because it is concealed by early retirement schemes, the granting of disability rather than unemployment benefits, and low-paid part-time employment.

3. The variation in unemployment experience in Europe

> "High regional and structural differences in unemployment make it so difficult to mobilize politically against unemployment." (Michele Salvati, at the Mallorca meeting of the Commission)

Unemployment rates differ widely from country to country (see Table 1). These differences partly reflect divergent policy responses to economic recession. Countries have varied both in the scope available to macroeconomic policy to maintain employment and in the political will to use it. The decline in employment has also been met by different labour market policies. Higher public employment, repatriation of foreign workers, early retirement schemes, easing of conditions for disability pensions and discrimination against women have all been used to lower open unemployment. In some countries official jobless rates have also been reduced by redefining the concept of unemployment.

All countries were hit by the economic crises which followed the two oil price shocks of 1973-74 and 1979. The national peculiarities show up in the way in which the repercussions were felt in the labour market. For instance, unemployment in the six EFTA countries has

TABLE 1. *Unemployment in the OECD area, 1973–90*

	% of total labour force					
	1973	1979	1983	1987	1988	1990
USA	4.9	5.8	9.6	6.2	5.5	5.5
Japan	1.3	2.1	2.7	2.8	2.5	2.5
Germany	1.0	3.3	8.2	7.9	7.8	7.8
France	2.7	6.0	8.4	10.5	10.3	10.8
United Kingdom	2.1	4.5	11.2	10.3	8.5	8.0
Italy	5.9	7.2	9.2	11.0	11.3	11.5
Canada	5.5	7.4	11.9	8.9	7.8	7.5
Austria	1.0	1.7	3.8	3.8	3.8	3.8
Belgium	2.3	7.3	12.9	11.2	10.5	9.8
Denmark	1.0	6.2	10.4	7.8	8.5	9.5
Finland	2.5	6.0	5.4	5.1	4.8	4.8
Greece	2.0	1.9	7.9	7.4	7.5	8.0
Ireland	5.7	7.1	14.0	17.7	16.5	16.0
Netherlands	3.1	5.6	15.0	12.6	12.5	12.5
Norway	1.6	2.0	3.4	2.0	3.0	3.8
Portugal	2.2	8.2	7.9	7.1	6.5	6.3
Spain	2.2	8.6	18.2	20.5	19.5	18.0
Sweden	2.0	1.7	2.9	1.9	1.8	2.0
Switzerland	0.0	0.3	0.8	0.7	0.8	0.8
Turkey	12.6	13.6	16.1	15.2	15.5	17.0
OECD Europe	3.5	6.1	10.4	10.7	10.3	10.3
Total OECD	3.5	5.4	8.9	7.9	7.3	7.5

Source: OECD

been far lower than in the European Community. In 1987, EFTA unemployment averaged about 3 per cent compared with about 11 per cent in the European Community. But one EFTA country—Switzerland—had a bad employment record in Europe after 1973, despite practically no official unemployment. Many foreign workers were obliged to leave the country, and women dropped out of the labour force.

By contrast, the three Nordic members of EFTA- —Norway, Sweden, and Finland—have dealt more successfully with unemployment. Not only are jobless rates lower, but participation rates also increased and are the highest in Europe. Austria too has performed well with respect to unemployment, though participation rates are not as high as in Scandinavia (See Figure 1).

Generally speaking, in "consensus" countries, inflation has been tackled by moderate wage claims and not by restrictive macroeconomic policies, a strategy aided by their systems of centralized wage bargaining. These countries differ from the rest of Europe, not in having greater flexibility in their economic systems and labour markets, but in the consensus across the political spectrum that unemployment is a social evil and a liability. The protection of employment is seen as a social goal which has popular support. These countries have also had quite a good economic performance. Their success is founded on a social system which relies on consensus rather than on class struggle. Employers and trade unions are often trying to solve problems together and are not simply defending well-established rights. Where trade unions are involved in major economic decisions —as in the three Nordic countries and Austria—they tend to feel responsible not just for their members, but for the health of the whole economy and for the unemployed.

In many European countries trade union resistance to lay-offs and their demands for government subsidies to ailing industries may conflict with necessary structural

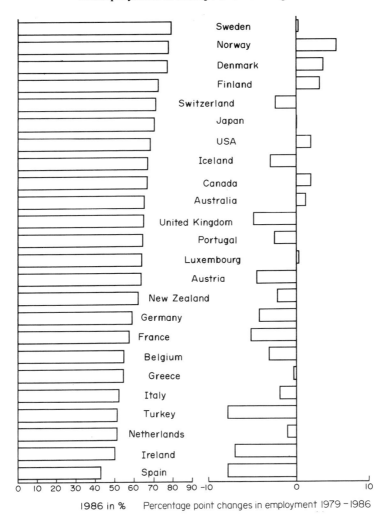

FIGURE 1. Employment/population ratio in 1986 and percentage changes, 1979–86: OECD countries

adjustment of the economy. But this resistance is weakened where unions have confidence in a long-term full employment policy. In Sweden and Finland, for example, society puts more emphasis on labour market security than on job security. In other words, workers are assured of the opportunity for employment but do not have a social right to remain in a particular job. Low unemployment could be compatible with few people changing jobs, but the consequence would be low income levels and poor international competitiveness. The EFTA countries have chosen to combine labour market security with rapid structural adjustment.

In southern Europe, official unemployment rates are often much higher than in northern Europe. In Spain, for instance, 21 per cent of the labour force and 39 per cent of young people are unemployed. In addition participation rates are much lower in the South, with the result that family income is further depressed. Low participation rates—reflecting lack of jobs—are at least as serious a problem as open unemployment. Nevertheless, utter misery is avoided by public welfare and "family insurance" of a more traditional type. The labour market situation in Italy and also in Spain is further obscured by a large "black economy", which provides more employment than officially recorded but in unregulated, often precarious jobs.

Regional differences in unemployment rates in southern Europe are more mixed than in northern Europe, often concentrated on young people and women. For a young girl in southern Italy the chance of finding employment is minimal. Yet the political repercussions are more muted than might be expected. Many of these regions have never in fact experienced a period of full employment. They have not been touched by an endogenous process of industrialization seen elsewhere in Europe, which created jobs on a large scale and generated a self-sustaining industrial and commercial culture. They do not know what they should ask for politically.

The fact that the incidence of unemployment in southern European countries is so unequal between areas, age and sex groups makes it more difficult to gain widespread popular support for remedial action, despite extremely high jobless rates for some groups.

Throughout Europe, the "inequalities of growth" show up in regional inequalities. Regional disparities in unemployment are marked. Within the European Community, unemployment rates in the 25 worst-affected regions are four times as high as in the 25 most prosperous. The regions with the highest unemployment rates are concentrated in Spain, Ireland, southern Italy and the north of the United Kingdom (see Figure 2). Regional disparities are greatest in Italy, Greece, the United Kingdom and, to a lesser extent, in West Germany.

The problems are most severe in two different types of region—"smokestack" areas and underdeveloped areas (particularly in the south of Europe). In Germany, for example, unemployment is very high in the northern regions (up to 15 per cent) which were once dominated by now-declining industries such as steel and shipbuilding. In south Germany, where there has been a new wave of high-tech industrialization, there is more or less full employment. The situation is very similar in the United Kingdom and other countries; regional differences in unemployment rates are increasing because long-term unemployment in depressed areas is proving very intractable, even where special regional policies are in operation.

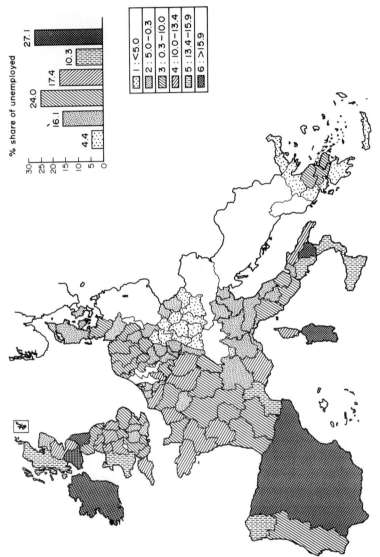

FIGURE 2. Regional unemployment rates in the European Community, 1986

4. Youth unemployment

"Today's youth unemployment may pose a threat to tomorrow's democracy." (Bruno Kreisky, at the first Vienna meeting of the Commission)

"There are two reactions to the aggressiveness of young people: the first is police, the second is to create adequate jobs for young people." (Clas-Erik Odhner, at the second Vienna meeting of the Commission)

Whereas the young were the winners in the 1960s boom, they were the main losers from Europe's poor economic performance in the early 1980s (see Table 2). Over one in five of Europe's young people are unemployed, roughly double the rate for adults. Older people who retire are often not replaced, while a recruitment freeze is regarded as a proven means to protect the already employed from the threat of redundancy. Early retirement and subsidies to ailing industries may keep open adult unemployment within bounds. But cuts in recruitment are rarely offset by other measures, with the result that in most countries unemployment rates for youngsters are far above average. There is a danger that many young people will never experience fruitful participation in society through regular employment; they will thus remain outside the mainstream of national life. This is simply unacceptable, politically, economically and morally.

A few countries have managed to keep youth unemployment rates close to those for adults, notably West Germany with its dual apprenticeship system (in which youngsters train partly in school and partly in firms). Austria and Scandinavia also have low youth unemployment. But while total employment has increased in most European countries since 1981, youth employment has

TABLE 2. *Youth unemployment*[1]

	% of total youth labour force			
	1973	1979	1983	1987
USA	9.9	11.3	16.4	11.9
Japan	2.3	3.4	4.5	5.2
Germany	0.9	3.4	10.7	7.9
France	(4.0)	(13.3)	19.7	23.0
United Kingdom	3.1	10.3	23.4	17.4
Italy	–	25.6	30.5	35.5
Austria	1.7	1.9	5.1	6.7
Finland	4.5	10.8	10.5	9.0
Netherlands	2.8	8.1	24.9	18.9
Norway	5.6	6.6	9.4	5.3
Spain	4.8	21.1	38.7	38.9
Sweden	5.2	5.0	8.0	4.2
Portugal	–	17.8	18.3	13.7

Source: OECD, WIFO
[1]Age group 15–24 or 16–24

continued to decline. In many countries the youth unemployment rate doubled in the first half of the 1980s, though special labour market programmes and more rapid economic growth have since prevented a further increase.

The "excluded" are to a large extent those boys and girls who leave school early with no formal qualifications and often little education for work. Functional illiteracy seems to be on the increase in several countries. But apprentices too sometimes end up among the excluded, especially if they cannot find work in the occupations for which they were trained. The problem is particularly acute for girls and young migrants who often move in and out of temporary jobs which have no future and give little social protection.

Two long-term trends exacerbate the problems for untrained young people: a reduction in jobs for the unskilled and a large inflow of women competing for unskilled work. The baby boom, by increasing the supply of young labour, has also contributed to high youth unemployment rates. It is to be hoped that the new generation entering the labour market in the 1990s will be in a better position, barring a deterioration in the general employment situation.

5. Long-term unemployment

"Once people fall out of the system, it is a tragedy that it is very difficult for them to get back." (James Gass, at the Paris meeting of the Commission)

"The problems of urban decay, poverty, single-parent families and long-term unemployment are closely interrelated." (John Evans, at the London meeting of the Commission)

Apart from youth unemployment, long-term unemployment is of central concern (see Table 3). Long-term unemployment creates a category of people who are caught in a vicious circle. They are stigmatized as hardship cases whom employers are reluctant to hire as long as there is strong competition for jobs.

In Europe, there is a core of long-term unemployed consisting to a large extent of those without adequate skills, people laid off in "smokestack" industries and living in remote areas, handicapped persons and so on. Some are not even always counted as unemployed in

TABLE 3. *Long-term unemployment*[1]

	% total of unemployment	
	1980	1987
Austria	9.2	10.8
Belgium	57.9	68.9[2]
Finland	27.0	14.8
France	32.6	45.5
Germany	17.0	32.0[2]
Ireland	34.8	44.4
Italy	37.1	56.4[3]
Netherlands	25.9	55.6
Norway	2.3	6.7[2]
Spain	34.5	61.9
Sweden	5.5	8.1
United Kingdom	19.2	42.6

Source: OECD

[1] 12 months and over   [2] 1986   [3] 1985

official statistics because they have given up actively looking for a job. Many may have applied for a hundred jobs without success.

Apart from open and registered unemployment there is also a large group of "marginal workers". This group is not continuously unemployed, but is permanently threatened by unemployment. Both the long-term unemployed and marginal workers could be helped by training programmes, a theme to which we return in our proposals.

About half the unemployed in Europe have been out of work for over a year. Generally, long-term unemployment increases with age. However, the proportion of older workers in long-term unemployment has fallen almost everywhere, mainly reflecting early retirement schemes and discouragement.

The share of youth in long-term unemployment has been increasing in those countries where total unemployment is still rising. The proportion of unemployed women has been declining as they have dropped out of the labour force, discouraged by lack of job opportunities.

Many long-term unemployed have been out of work for over two years (about half in Belgium, one-third in Spain and one-quarter in Great Britain and France). Not only are these people demoralized and impoverished, but their vocational skills have been impaired, worsening their chances of re-employment. The loss of skills is the greatest risk of long-term unemployment.

6. Unemployment among women

"Unemployment threatens equal treatment of women." (Paavo Lipponen, at the Helsinki meeting of the Commission)

"Women increasingly want to have an occupation. This calls for more nursery and all-day-schools." (Jean Kaspar, at the Paris meeting of the Commission)

In most European countries, unemployment among women is higher than among men. There is a danger that sluggish labour market conditions may be reinforcing discrimination against women, on the presumption that women live in households with more than one income-earner. Unemployment among women lowers family incomes—often the wife's earnings are essential to keep families out of poverty—and wastes valuable productive resources.

Official statistics usually understate female unemployment. Married women who are not searching actively for a job are to a large extent excluded. However, they tend to show up on the labour market as soon as employment opportunities increase. Many new jobs in the service sector, often part-time, have gone to married women, reducing disguised unemployment rather than the open unemployment recorded by official statistics.

During the last decade, female employment has grown rapidly as part-time work in service has expanded. But full-time job opportunities in the industrial sector have declined for women as well as men, while demographic factors and rising female participation rates have boosted women's unemployment. Demographic factors will ease the labour market situation in the future but the rise in participation rates is likely to continue. Higher levels of education and continuation of work after marriage and/or child-bearing are the crucial elements in this socioeconomic development.

As a result of the industrial crisis—the decline of employment in "smokestack" industries and mass production—men's jobs were hit harder than women's because men accounted for a high proportion of industrial employment. But looking at unemployment figures does not give the full picture. In Switzerland, for instance, female participation rates declined in recessions. It was politically and socially accepted that wives should stay at home when jobs were scarce. In Sweden and Norway, unemployment remained fairly low at the same time as there was a massive increase in part-time work by married women.

7. Social consequences of unemployment

"The broken tie to the larger social unit is the main psychological burden of unemployment." (Marie Jahoda, at the London meeting of the Commission)

"A society that does not consistently offer meaningful, productive and remunerative job opportunities to all who are willing to work cannot avoid social instability. Unemployment benefits and social welfare payments, though necessary, cannot recompense for the meaningless, worthlessness, insecurity and isolation, which result from a fruitless job search—with social polarization and fragmentation among the consequences." (Statement by BIAC and TUAC, the employer and trade union advisory committees to the OECD)[3]

When mass unemployment hits millions, as it has done now for the second time in this century, the consequences are above all on the living standards of those affected. During the great depression of the 1930s the unemployed lived in abject poverty. In many cases, private charity was the only means to prevent starvation. In the enormous economic, social and political changes of the last 50 years, state support for the unemployed has become the rule. Though the degree of financial support varies considerably between countries, the standard of living of today's unemployed is considerably higher than it was in the 1930s. However, in many countries, unemployment benefits have been reduced during the 1980s in the name of curbing budget deficits and creating stronger incentives for active job search. The long-term unemployed commonly find their entitlements to benefits running out and others, unable to satisfy qualifying conditions, are also outside the entitlement system. Both are obliged to rely on low levels of public relief.

Unemployment nevertheless creates less political resistance than in the past, partly because the household structure of unemployment has changed. In contrast to the 1930s, many jobless are assumed to live in households with more than one breadwinner and receive unemployment benefits or welfare payments. In Austria, one-third of the unemployed are young people living with their parents and one-third are wives of heads of households. Only about ten per cent of all unemployed are heads of households who have to support a family. In other countries, however, such as Great Britain, jobless people often live in households where all the members are unemployed.

Even if only a relatively small proportion of jobless workers are family breadwinners, that should not mean that unemployment no longer merits political pride of place. Unemployment is damaging for the individual, a major cause of poverty amid affluence, and corrosive for society in its denial of full citizenship rights to a large minority.

Many governments do not take full account of the real costs of unemployment, which consist of much more than the loss of potential output. There are psycho-social consequences of unemployment (sickness, mental illness, and so on) that should not be underestimated. There are also high macroeconomic costs—not only in additional unemployment benefits, but also in lost taxes and social security contributions. The cost to society of employing more people is thus far smaller than conventional calculations sometimes suggest.

For the individual, the impact of unemployment is immediate and increases with time. Unemployment of today's youth is a humiliation of the new generation with consequences that will last for decades.

The social and psychological consequences of being unemployed show remarkable similarities over time and between countries. It is this similarity in the tragic repetition of mass misery that makes it possible to disentangle to some extent the consequences of poverty from those of losing a job.

Employment is organized in a way that enforces a time-structure on the day; it enlarges the scope of social experience into areas that are less emotionally charged than family life, but are socially and cognitively more informative. It demonstrates that modern life requires collective efforts. It also makes obvious the necessity of rules and regulations. Jointly these categories of experience operate to tie people into the social web.

When unemployment strikes, these categories of experience are no longer institutionally enforced and the tie to the larger social unit is broken. The sense of being excluded, not needed, without purposeful activity and isolated from others, constitutes the psychological burden of unemployment. Unlimited time is not leisure but boredom.

A serious problem is posed by discrimination against immigrants, including those of the second generation. Immigrants or foreign workers are more severely hit by unemployment than the native populations, and are sometimes accused of adding to unemployment. Immigrant children in some regions of Europe live in a hostile environment that provokes racial tension and aggression. This is one of the great dangers of unemployment.

On the social level, an underclass is created, separated from the majority by mutual hostility and demoralization. In the 1930s the disaster of unemployment was conquered in Central Europe by the war preparations of national socialism. Totalitarian organizations then met to some extent the same needs that, under ordinary circumstances, are satisfied by holding a job.

Rowdyism and vandalism by youngsters represent a violent response to feelings of rejection and alienation which are reinforced by labour market inequalities. Tougher policing is no solution. The answer has to be the creation of jobs.

Study after study has documented that the unemployed want jobs, not hand-outs that offend their dignity. Thousands of long-term unemployed do not seek social income support even though they are entitled to receive it. Several studies of long-term unemployment in Finland support the commonsense notion that unemployment is a crisis for the individual, causing passivity and loss of life-perspective. There was no general increase in alcoholism or obvious family problems. On the contrary, family ties were strengthened. However, a British study found that the mortality rate of the wives of men seeking work was some 20 per cent higher than that of other married women, while a Swedish study discovered that the children of unemployed people had significantly greater health problems. Thus it is not only the unemployed themselves who are affected but also their families, involving the next generation.

Various studies show that the psychological effects of unemployment depend heavily on people's network of social contacts. Those with family and other supporting contacts suffer less psychological damage. Thus women are often less affected than men, while single men without relatives or friends are particularly vulnerable. There is a high incidence of alcoholism in this latter category.

The material consequences of unemployment are only

partly—and to a declining extent—alleviated by social welfare even in many of the more affluent, highly industrialized countries. The psychological effects of unemployment remain an unsolved problem, which worsens during extended periods of unemployment. Unemployment is a corrosive experience for most people. The picture of the unemployed as wealthy "dole scroungers" could not be further from the truth.

Some people argue that the unemployed should find satisfaction in voluntary work and be the bearers of a new culture in which paid work is no longer a central feature. This is utopianism. Studies of the unemployed have shown that without work many lose their motivation to do anything.[4]

In the longer run the damage to attitudes and social morality from widespread unemployment may be even more serious. The democratic system is underpinned by a complex interlocking set of inculcated doctrines concerning civic responsibility and mutual respect. This foundation is undermined in a society which does not accept responsibility for many of its citizens and shows them scant respect.

Unemployment may not provoke political revolution. But, as in the 1930s, it can engender apathy and readiness to join authoritarian organizations. Unemployment also weakens rather than strengthens the ability of trade unions to act as a political focus for discontent. Thus the risk is not a large-scale confrontation, but erosion of the foundations of society itself.

The reasons for fighting unemployment are therefore not only concern for the unemployed and their families as individuals, but also the threat that unemployment poses to the rest of society. Moreover, the enforced idleness of some lowers living standards for everyone in the community because productive resources are going unused. Bringing those resources back to work will be of benefit to all.

Part II: Why Has
Unemployment Risen?

1. Our argument

> "A large part of unemployment in Europe is due to a defi-
> ciency of demand." (Stephen Potter, at the Paris meeting of
> the Commission)

High unemployment in Europe in the 1980s has been the
result of government responses to the structural crisis
that hit their economies in the 1970s. Restrictive economic policies, intended primarily to restrain inflation
and to teach trade unions a lesson, lowered growth and
raised unemployment. This happened at a time when
labour supply was growing rapidly, as the baby-boom
generation entered the job market and more women
sought paid work. In these circumstances higher investment was called for. Instead investment faltered.

Governments failed to cope adequately with structural
changes—the need to reduce dependence on expensive oil
and other fuels, intensified competition from Japan and
the newly industrializing countries and so on—partly
because national solutions were no longer effective or
appropriate. Increased international interdependence
means that the standard national economic policy levers

31

do not work as they once did. They can even be counter-productive, as was demonstrated in the early 1980s when much of Europe adopted deflationary policies which together plunged the region into slump. The need for policy co-ordination between countries is discussed in a later section on international constraints to expansionary policies.

Structural change has meant that the rise in unemployment has been closely linked with the decline in industrial employment, concentrated on industry-specific skills and in certain declining areas where job opportunities for the young have virtually disappeared. The increase of service jobs in urban centres, often requiring specific skills or offering only part-time work, has not been a real offset for the shake-out of industrial jobs elsewhere. Thus tackling unemployment involves not only faster economic growth but also measures to ease structural change and help back into work those who would otherwise be left behind.

Some people believe that unemployment has risen because of high productivity increases that are inevitable in the course of technical progress. According to this view, employment must fall as human work is replaced by machines. Like so many conclusions from everyday life, this line of argument does not hold for the whole economy. Society's wants and demands are constantly changing and increasing as higher productivity generates additional wealth and spending power. In fact, in the past decade, productivity growth has been only half that in the earlier postwar period, yet mass unemployment has soared.

Others argue that Europe's economies are now running well, experiencing the longest upswing since the

TABLE 4. *Growth of GDP, employment and productivity, 1980–87*

	GDP-growth	Employment growth 1980–87 p.a. in %	Productivity growth
OECD Europe	+ 1.9	+ 0.2	+ 1.7
USA	+ 3.1	+ 1.8	+ 1.3
Japan	+ 3.7	+ 0.9	+ 2.8

Source: OECD

war. Thus there is no need for action to boost growth. Unemployment persists because of rigid labour markets. This view is not supported by the facts. The recent Brookings Institution study on the European economy, *Barriers to European Growth*,[5] paints a quite different and much darker picture. The European economy is not running well. In the 1980s, economic growth has been about half that in Japan and the United States (see Table 4). Since 1973 western Europe has steadily lost ground in world markets. While the region has a large current account surplus, this is the consequence of restricting domestic demand rather than a high level of competitiveness. Sluggish economic growth averaging about $2\frac{1}{2}$ per cent is not enough to improve the labour market situation. It is merely keeping pace with productivity growth. The higher growth rates of the last two years are considered by forecasters to be only temporary.

2. The importance of economic growth for employment

In the 1960s and early 1970s Europe's growth rate averaged nearly 5 per cent a year, employment was rising and

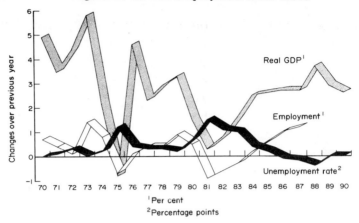

FIGURE 3. Rates of change in economic activity:
OECD Europe, 1970–90

unemployment rates oscillated around 2 per cent. Infla-
tion rates did not exceed $3\frac{1}{2}$ per cent, but were rising at the
end of the period. Real interest rates were sometimes
negative.

Since the first oil crisis of 1973-74, Europe seems to
have been caught in a slow-growth trap. From 1973 to
1987, economic growth averaged barely 2 per cent in real
terms. The United States did a little better at $2\frac{1}{2}$ per cent,
while Japan managed almost 4 per cent. Employment
rose by 2 per cent annually in the United States and 1 per
cent in Japan, but in Europe the number of jobs
remained virtually unchanged throughout the entire period. As a result, the growing labour supply could not be
accommodated, and there was a corresponding rise in
unemployment, from 5.5 million in 1973 to 19 million in
1987.

Figure 3 amply demonstrates the link between economic growth and employment. High growth rates have
been accompanied by an increase in employment, low
growth rates by a decrease. There is also a fairly close

relationship between economic growth and employment in an international cross-section analysis. In general, countries with higher economic or industrial growth experienced faster employment growth.

However, there are two notable exceptions to this generalization. In North America, employment growth has been higher than would be expected from economic growth. Additional employment in the low wage sector has been identified as a main element in this development.

In "consensus countries" (Sweden, Norway, Finland) employment also rose faster than their growth performance might suggest, due—at least in the 1970s—to a rapid expansion of public employment. The statistical relation between the growth of production and employment does not mean that the first simply determines the latter. A policy for employment promotion will enhance production as well.

Some people believe that the impact of economic growth on employment has diminished (or even vanished) in recent years. Calculations by the European Commission indicate, on the contrary, that growth has become more employment-creating in Europe. While the threshold above which an increase can be expected was equivalent to an annual increase in GDP of over 4 per cent before 1973, the corresponding figure was just over 2 per cent in the period 1973-79 and below 2 per cent in the period 1979-87. (Even adjusted to take account of increased part-time work, this picture is not altered significantly.) Above the threshold the rise in employment is roughly half the additional growth rate, because a higher level of demand stimulates higher productivity, as UK experiences demonstrates.

A rate of less than 3 per cent in Europe, as predicted by the OECD for 1990, will make little or no contribution to reducing the high level of unemployment. Even if growth were $3\frac{1}{2}$ per cent, which presently seems to be a possibility, unemployment will at best be reduced by only half a percentage point. With the continuing expansion of labour supply until the mid-1990s, there is a danger that unemployment will rise further, especially if the economy moves into recession. A growing proportion of jobless would be long-term unemployed or young people who have never worked, at risk of becoming a group permanently detached from the rest of society.

Part III: An Economic Programme for Europe

1. Macroeconomic strategies: the big push

"Changing the present unemployment situation and achieving full employment through more investments and higher economic growth should ... be the main objective of economic and social policy." (Statement by BIAC and TUAC, the employer and trade union advisory committees to the OECD).[6]

"High unemployment in Europe is no act of God, governments can do much more about it than they did in the last decade." (Willem Buiter, at the London meeting of the Commission)

Europe needs fast growth to achieve a significant reduction of unemployment sustained over a number of years. A reasonable target would be to bring down the average unemployment rate in Western Europe by one percentage point a year. This would mean that between 1989 and 1995 the unemployment rate would be brought down to the level that existed in the late 1970s and that by 1995 unemployment would average around 5 per cent. Different countries would need different targets given the dispersal of European unemployment rates betwen 2 per cent and 21 per cent. But meeting the suggested average target would require annual employment growth of at least 1.5 per cent to allow for labour force expansion, including higher participation rates, as discouraged workers return to the labour market. This would mean the creation of about 2.5 million jobs each year in Western Europe. In total, the creation of about 15 million jobs by 1995 would be required.

Although it would be wrong to take a mechanistic view of the relationship between employment growth, GDP growth and productivity, it is clear that achieving this jobs target would involve annual growth rates of at least $3\frac{1}{2}$ per cent for several years. Current OECD forecasts that European growth may again decline to $2\frac{1}{2}$ per cent in 1990 are therefore deeply disturbing.

Growth is not necessary primarily as a means of creating employment, but there are still vast unmet needs to be satisfied in Western Europe and even more so in the world as a whole, and it is neither realistic nor desirable to envisage meeting such needs solely through redistributing resources and income. The financing of pension systems to support ageing populations, as well as the debt problems of developing countries, become critical if average growth falls below 3 per cent a year for a long period.

However, the quality of growth is as important as its level. The beneficial effects of growth need to be equitably distributed. Economic expansion must not be allowed to take place at the expense of the environment or exhaust limited natural resources. It needs to result in an improvement in the quality of life. The Brundtland Commission report[7] was right in emphasizing that it is the content of growth rather than its level which determines its environmental impact. Zero growth with mass unemployment will not help the environment. Faster growth through investment can serve both ecological and economic purposes. We are concerned to "twist" the nature of growth by advocating programmes which are environmentally benign and widen the distribution of the benefits of expansion.

Ensuring adequate growth of the right kind is neither a matter of simple demand management nor of "leaving it to the market". There has been some recognition in the lastest policy debates, at least tacitly, that fiscal and monetary policy does have a role to play in ensuring that economic capacity is being used to the maximum, while structural policies are needed to ensure that capacity is expanding. Despite increased company profits and liquidity, investment in productive assets has remained inadequate. The present surge in productive investments is unfortunately not expected to continue. High profits on financial investments detract managers' interest from productive ones.

Neither the free market nor the labour flexibility strategies pursued during the last decade have succeeded in reducing unemployment for Europe as a whole. Economic policy, aided by tumbling commodity prices, has achieved lower inflation but the promised growth and employment which was supposed to follow has not materialized.

We do not accept the widely prevalent view that, in the medium term, unemployment cannot be influenced by expansionary economic policies. This view, which holds that such strategies would lead only to higher inflation and government indebtedness, not to lower unemployment, is based on mistaken assumptions, as we argue later. The present unemployment situation is neither inevitable nor acceptable. Those countries which have had the political will and social cohesion to fight unemployment have shown that there is a way out even within the present system.

Expansion in the context of the internal market of the European Community

> "Working people will simply not understand, nor accept, all the structural changes that the internal market will produce if they only learn about them when being shown the door." (Peter Coldrick, at the London meeting of the Commission)

> "The completion of the internal market necessitates regulations that prevent social dumping." (Mathias Hinterscheid, at the London meeting of the Commission)

The European Community has set itself the task of building a barrier-free internal market by the end of 1992, which will entail resolving such thorny issues as harmonization of indirect taxes and technical norms, creation of a common market for public procurement, elimination of non-tariff trade barriers, and so on. It is the most ambitious task of the Community since its very beginnings, demanding comprehensive adjustments but also providing important opportunities for increased efficiency and higher living standards.

Creating the large internal market for 320 million consumers is a major challenge for Europe, not only for the members of the European Community, but also for EFTA and COMECON countries. Co-operation between EC and EFTA countries will need to be strengthened.

One of the aims of the internal market is to enable

European economies to stand up to competition from the United States and Japan. The sharpening of international competition calls for closer co-ordination. There is some hope that the large "market without frontiers" can help restore Europe's economic health and serve as an engine of economic growth. Economies of scale and more competition may lead to an increase in productivity and downward pressure on prices, particularly in the service sector and those industries now protected by non-tariff barriers.

According to a recent study—the Cecchini Report[8]—the economic gains from the 1992 programme could be $4\frac{1}{4}$ per cent to $6\frac{1}{2}$ per cent of GDP and about 2 million to 5 million jobs (see Table 5). It could also increase productivity by 0.5 per cent a year, which would reduce the employment effect of growth accordingly. In spite of supply-side effects and economies of scale, however, we doubt that the completion of the internal market alone will be sufficient to revive the European economy. Even if the higher figure of five million additional jobs was achieved, which would require more expansionary policies to stimulate growth and investment, that would still leave over ten million jobless in the EC alone. The EC Commission has itself stressed that the full benefits of market integration will not be reaped unless there are more expansionary policies to stimulate growth and investment. We will develop this issue much further in the section on international constraints.

In 1985, the Commission of the European Community put forward a co-operative growth strategy designed to achieve an annual growth rate of 3 to $3\frac{1}{2}$ per cent to reduce unemployment in Europe to an acceptable level by the mid-1990s and to ensure the success of the internal

TABLE 5. *Potential consequences of completion of the internal market for the Community in the medium/long term*

	GDP (% change)	Prices (% change)	Employment increase (in millions)	Public balance improvement (% of GDP)	External balance improvement (% of GDP)
Without accompanying measures[1]	$+4\frac{1}{2}$	-6	$+1\frac{3}{4}$	$+2\frac{1}{4}$	$+1$
With accompanying measures[1]	$+7$	$-4\frac{1}{2}$	$+5$	$+\frac{1}{2}$	$-\frac{1}{4}$

Source: Cecchini Report
[1]Margin of error ±30%

market exercise. This strategy, which we strongly support, was endorsed by the European employers' organization (UNICE) and by the European trade unions (ETUC), as well as by the Council of Ministers, though unfortunately in practice it has been largely ignored by governments. Experience shows, however, that the growth target must be set higher to achieve the stated goal.

According to the Cecchini study, completion of the internal market will lead to a tremendous increase in the average size of the enterprises in the Community. This implies mergers and the death of many small firms. Thus a strong competition policy is needed to ensure that the benefits of a barrier-free market are not thwarted by monopolistic practices. In addition, structural policies are needed to exploit fully the potential advantages of the large market. Small and medium-sized enterprises must be enabled to meet its challenges. The internal market must also work for the benefit of the less advantaged areas, which may not gain from it in the short term. Regional or structural funds should be made available to improve the necessary infrastructure in these regions.

Business organizations and trade unions have welcomed the creation of the internal market. Trade unions, however, stress that there need to be social measures to accompany economic measures. There are two channels for promotion of this social dimension: European social legislation and the dialogue between the social partners at the European level.

The Commission has argued that the creation of the internal market must go hand in hand with the creation of a "European social area". There must be at least minimum community-wide social regulations concerning working conditions. The Beretta Report[9] puts it very clearly: "The beneficial effects of a large market would be dissipated if some member States were to seek a competitive advantage by sacrificing social achievements." The ETUC has stressed the need for regulations to prevent "social dumping" practices, though this has been resisted by the employers' organization (UNICE), which is afraid of creating new labour market rigidities.

Another aspect that must be tackled is the harmonization of national health and accident insurance regulations.

One of the social prerequisites for the completion of the internal market is that it promotes the creation of jobs. Employment must be at the core of social policy. Closer co-ordination between European countries may make it easier to organize cross-border investment in infrastructure and environmental protection (see below).

Expansion in a world and pan-European context

"We need more than 3½ per cent annual economic growth for a few years in Europe over a few years to cut unemployment. But every time we approach 2½ per cent growth, national banks and governments endeavour to cool down the overheating economy by raising interest rates." (Ewald Walterskirchen, at the second Vienna meeting of the Commission)

"I am convinced that lower real interest rates would have much positive influence on the growth of the economy." (Ferdinando Borletti, Italian industrialist, at the Mallorca meeting of the Commission)

Against a background of massive trade and other imbalances, economic policies worldwide have lost credibility. Of the three main scenarios for correcting trade imbalances, two should be avoided at all costs: a deep recession in the United States or a further pronounced fall in the dollar would do lasting damage to the world economy and hence to Europe's growth prospects. Economic adjustment to eliminate global payments imbalances would be best achieved by faster growth of domestic demand in Japan and Europe, which are running large surpluses, than by restrictions in the United States.

The United States made an important contribution to world economic recovery and prevention of a debt crisis when domestic demand was boosted after August 1982 by tax reductions, higher public expenditures (though mainly for armament) and by a more relaxed, accommodating monetary policy. While Europe as a "free-rider" reaped benefits from this programme, the US economy is now suffering the consequences in the form of a massive trade deficit.

Under US pressure, Japan has effectively implemented a fiscal programme to boost internal demand in recent years. Now it is up to Europe to make a contribution to the world economy.

Europe cannot expect further external growth impulses in the medium term. The international adjustment process will undoubtedly take several years, and requires a higher growth rate of internal demand in Europe if economic expansion and employment are not to be adversely affected. In other words, stronger internal growth has to make a key contribution to eliminating international imbalances and bringing about an appreciable and lasting reduction in unemployment.

Headroom for expansion exists in macroeconomic

policy. It is true that because of the high degree of interdependence of the European economies, some individual countries' attempts in the past to expand unilaterally (for example, France) very soon came up against external trade and fiscal constraints and had to be abandoned. Others (the Nordic countries, Austria) have been more successful.

But the appropriate conclusion is not that expansionary policies are ineffective, but that they should be broadly designed and co-ordinated internationally. Monetary, fiscal and wage policies as well as long-run supply-side policies must all be harnessed in the quest for growth, employment and stability. Indeed, they tend to reinforce each other. For instance, the more wage policy is successful in creating conditions for a steadier trend in prices, the more expansionary monetary and fiscal policies can be. (We deal with the international and inflation constraints in Part V.)

Co-ordination of policies at the national and international level is also necessary to ensure their consistency and efficacy. At the national level, proposals for such co-ordination are neither new nor lacking in number. In West Germany, they were institutionalized in 1967, in the shape of the law to promote growth and stability. This "concerted action" collapsed in 1977. However, such an approach still holds sway in a number of Western European countries. New impetus was given to the concept of co-ordination at the international level by the European Commission's proposal for a co-operative growth strategy which accepted that economic policy co-ordination at the national level is no longer sufficient in an interdependent and increasingly integrated Europe. International co-ordination would reduce the external and budgetary constraints that hamper the pursuit of expansionary policies and, in particular, would give those countries with limited or no room for manoeuvre fresh scope for action. This in turn would promote the growth process generally. As a result, a mutually reinforcing virtuous circle would be possible.

Recent economic summits of the seven leading Western economies show that international policy co-ordination has made some progress regarding stabilization of currencies and remedying trade balances, but unemployment has not even been a point of debate.

Economic policy must be designed in such a way as to be sustainable in the medium term. It is not therefore a question of pulling out all the stops in an uncontrolled attempt to engineer short-term growth. Such action would meet with little success, since it would not impress firms or consumers. It is necessary to improve the prospects for growth in a lasting manner. This means that the programmes start by creating the jobs and training the unemployed to perform them. The multiplier effect will then spread employment to other sectors.

Some governments have been reluctant to aim for faster economic expansion, fearing a resurgence of inflation more than persistent joblessness. But there is a long way to go in most European countries before an expansionary economic policy would come up against an inflationary constraint, and this risk can be further reduced by income and labour market policy.

To reiterate, it is indeed possible to end the unemployment crisis in Europe, if governments and the social partners show the will to co-operate. Unemployment is extremely costly. Europe is not rich enough to afford it. There are still enormous needs to be met.

A "European way"

"As much market as possible, as much planning as necessary." (Edgar Plan, at the Mallorca meeting of the Commission)

"We need 'competitive' economic growth, only that kind of growth is lasting." (Raymond Barre, former French Prime Minister, at the Paris meeting of the Commission)

The focus of this report is on European unemployment, but the solution does not lie in selfish and autarkic policies. For us a "European way" means a civilized, fully employed Europe in a peaceful, rapidly developing and ecologically conscious world. In this context, Europe should tackle the unemployment problem by directing resources in accordance with its own priorities. We consider the three most important to be:

— an ecologically safe world for its citizens, their children and grandchildren;
— a full utilization of the educational and intellectual potential of the population in order to meet the scientific and cultural challenges of our times and shape a culturally richer and more humane society; and
— a more even spread of material well-being within and between countries, and particularly between North and South.

Not casino capitalism, but "tempered" capitalism is required to achieve these goals. The co-operation of industry, employers' associations, trade unions, governments and their agencies is crucial for success.

Those countries with a more consensus-oriented culture could point the way. Consensus-building is a cumulative process. A package of increased employment, higher real wages through lower nominal wage claims, more equitable distribution and improved working conditions would strengthen consensus and allow investment-led expansion to be pushed further.

Huge investment opportunities exist to be exploited, as we describe later in this report. Many of the projects we propose deal with the problems we see as priorities.

Improving physical and human infrastructure investment to increase employment and to stimulate private investment is preferable to tax cuts. The employment effects of additional public investment are far higher than those of tax cuts. Additional investment immediately increases effective demand whereas much of the net income gains through tax cuts is spent on imports or remains in savings accounts. Upper- and middle-class households who mainly benefit from lower marginal tax rates usually have high savings rates.

To quote the OECD Employment outlook 1986:[10]

> There may be little difference in the short-run employment effects between cutting employers' payroll taxes and other tax cuts. Both would be significantly less powerful in the short run than increase in public expenditure in generating an increase in employment.

Ten years ago, the OECD estimated that the net job-creating effect of an income tax cut (in the United States) was about half as great as the effect of increased public works.[11] This conclusion is confirmed by more recent studies.[12]

Today, a growing number of governments feel that the public sector has reached its tolerable limits. Thus, a combination of private and public effort is necessary. Certainly, public tasks need not be public expenditures.

An investment programme for Europe will ultimately be financed largely by higher tax revenues resulting from higher incomes and their multiplier effects. For a single country, "self-financing" ratios for investment are much lower because some of the spending is dissipated in imports. The success of the programme also depends on the reactions of private investors to increased demand and higher profits resulting from higher capacity utilization.

A programme for the 1990s

> "Also the OECD is increasingly concerned with environmental protection, education and training, as well as technology and innovation." (Pierre Vinde, at the Paris meeting of the Commission)

The Commission's report is not simply addressed to people interested in economic matters, because unemployment is not simply an economic problem. Our report is addressed to a larger audience: in particular it makes an appeal to people interested in ecology, culture, developing countries and social affairs, because recommendations to fight unemployment involve all these areas. A programme for more employment in Europe should contain the following elements:

— *Improving the European infrastructure.* The completion of the internal market calls for adequate infrastructure—good transport links between countries, high-speed rail tracks, efficient telecommunications, and so on. European disparities in infrastructure need to be reduced and a balance struck between the interests of different regions. The economic crisis has created new depressed areas in addition to the old ones. The gap between poor and rich regions in Europe needs to be reduced. In addition, our cities have lost their attractiveness. Urban renewal would make them nicer places in which to live. Europe also needs a better "social infrastructure": housing—particularly for the young—and care for the ageing population. These are immediate problems for many people.

— *Environmental protection.* This requires large-scale investment, both private and public. Only by taking environmental protection seriously can we blunt antipathy to economic growth. Pollution does not respect national frontiers, and is very severe in some Eastern European countries. There is an urgent need for technical and financial East-West co-operation to restore and preserve the European environment.

— *Culture and education.* It is not only the traditional working class that is affected by unemployment, but increasingly also young people in the field of culture (in the broadest sense of the word)—university graduates, teachers, high school graduates. While many young, well-educated people are without work, educational and cultural needs, particularly outside the cities, are not being satisfied. Cultural industries are obviously very labour- and skill-intensive.

— *Technology and innovation.* Europe's own technological potential must be strengthened in order to counteract dependence on overseas technology and to counteract any tendency to "Eurosclerosis". There is scope to increase the content of human skills in technology.

— *New service industries*. A great potential for increased employment lies in the service economy —particularly in producer services. These are often high-skill high-income jobs.

— *Development aid and East-West relations*. It is also in Europe's interest that Third World debt problems are solved and North–South and East–West relations are strengthened. Improved trade ties generate economic growth and employment. Much needs to be done in the developing countries. The opportunities for investment, which would benefit Europe as well as the rest of the world, are virtually unlimited.

Projects in these fields could help reorient or "twist" employment towards skilled jobs; this is most evident for a forward-looking strategy in technology, education and culture. But environmental protection and energy saving also require much research into new technologies, and involve the production of investment goods that require skilled labour. Urban and village renewal demands skilled (craft) work, and many of the new producer services offer very high-skilled jobs. More East-West and North–South trade would mean more exports with a high technological content, since that is what other countries seek from Europe. All this means an upgrading of the European labour force—in sharp contrast to the "flexibility strategy" that builds on low-wage and low-productivity jobs to reduce unemployment. An essential element of our strategy is the part to be played by training, in providing workers with new skills, and redeploying experienced workers, with suitable skill improvements, in more exacting jobs.

2. Improving the European infrastructure

"The tunnel under the Channel is a very good example of how private and public interests of different countries can be combined." (Alistair Morton, Co-Chairman of Eurotunnel, at the London meeting of the Commission)

The investment gap

Slow growth in Europe has been partly a consequence of low investment. The investment ratio (as a percentage of GDP) fell from 23.6 per cent in 1970 to 18.9 per cent in 1986. In Japan it rose in the 1980s from 30 per cent to 35 per cent of GDP. In the European manufacturing sector, the decline of capital-intensive industries (steel and the like) has been an important factor. The drop in investment has also been particularly pronounced in housing and in the public sector. Since investment has remained depressed for more than a decade, a yawning investment gap has opened up. If more jobs are to be created on a permanent basis, investment in Europe in the medium term will have to grow much faster than GDP. Capacity has been reduced by scrapping even relatively new investments so that the existing capital stock in most countries is not now sufficient for full employment. The investment growth of 1987-88 needs to continue.

While the scale and structure of public investment

depend directly on government policy, private investment, which accounts for some 85 per cent of total
investment, is determined essentially by profitability and
demand expectations.

The profitability of private investment in Europe has
improved appreciably in recent years. Higher capacity
utilization, the fall in the prices of key raw materials and,
in particular, the fact that real wage increases have not
kept pace with productivity gains for several years, have
meant that profits have risen significantly following the
setback at the beginning of the 1980s. This favourable
situation is, however, marred by historically high real
interest rates. Since 1984, long-term real interest rates
have hovered around 5 per cent, compared with 2 per
cent on average in the 1960s. A less restrictive monetary
policy stance, together with low inflationary expectations and progress towards elimination of international
imbalances, should permit a fall in long-term interest
rates. This would favourably influence investment
activity in the long run: financing costs would fall and the
relationship between the expected return on fixed assets
and financial assets would shift in favour of productive
investment in fixed assets. Lower long-term interest rates
would also take considerable pressure off public budgets,
adding to the room for manoeuvre.

In bringing about a significant increase in investment
activity, an improvement in demand prospects is at least
as important as a satisfactory level of profitability. As
argued earlier, this improvement will need to come from
domestic demand. Thus, fiscal policy must contribute
directly by expanding public investment or, in some
countries, through tax cuts, especially for low-income
families with a high propensity to consume.

The need for infrastructure investment

"A major lack of Southern Europe is the absence of basic infrastructure, in particular telecommunications." (Jose M. Escondrillas, at the Mallorca meeting of the Commission)

Modern economic history teaches that all major growth cycles were preceded by large infrastructure projects, particularly in transport (railways, highways). Today, the "transport" of information—telecommunications and computers—is of similar strategic importance. There is a large backlog of investment demand. Increased infrastructure investment would be a central means of achieving higher medium-term growth rates. There should be a closer collaboration between the public and the private sector on basic infrastructure projects. The challenge is to combine private and public money.

In the past, infrastructure investment was financed almost entirely through public funds. However, public investment has suffered from budget constraints in all European countries. Most countries did not intend to curtail public investment so heavily at the outset, but investment curbs proved to be the simplest way of stabilizing budgets. This decrease in infrastructure investment, which has also had negative effects on private investment, must be reversed.

At present, the European economies have excess capacity and are therefore in a position to carry out additional tasks. Much of Europe's infrastructure needs repair and upgrading, which have been neglected because of budget squeezes. It would not make sense to allow the highway and rail networks to expand at the same pace as in the past, but they need to be improved. Real resources, including unemployed labour, are available for new tasks, such as environmental protection, urban renewal, improved transportation facilities, and so on. Without new projects the building industry, despite the continuing demand for house construction in many parts of Europe, could be headed for a downturn.

The planned creation of an integrated European market, requiring appropriate infrastructure, opens up new prospects for the European building industry. We concur in the need for the investments that have been suggested by the EC Commission. We are also fully in agreement with the Round Table of European Industrialists which has suggested a large programme of infrastructure investment to the European Commission.[13]

Public tasks and private investment in infrastructure

"In many European countries, public investment (as per cent of GDP) is now half as high as in the early 1970s." (Claus Hofmann, at the London meeting of the Commission)

"A new relationship between private and public sector is needed." (James Gass, at the Paris meeting of the Commission)

Public and infrastructure investment not only influence demand in the economy but help to expand productive potential. They need to be geared to the medium term if they are to create a predictable framework. On the one hand, they can complement private investment and, on the other, they may open new areas of growth.

Public tasks need not be public expenditures, as we have said earlier. Stepping up public investment may nevertheless be necessary. The contraction in recent years

TABLE 6. *Public investment as a percentage of GDP, 1970 and 1986*

	1970	1986
Belgium	4.4	2.2
Germany	4.7	2.5
Denmark	5.1	1.8
France	3.9	3.6
Italy	3.0	3.6
Netherlands	5.0	2.3
Spain	2.6	3.6
United Kingdom	5.4	2.1

has been even more pronounced than for private investment. In most countries real public investment, as a proportion of GDP, has substantially declined over the last 15 years (see Table 6).

Apart from Italy and Spain, where public investment actually rose as a proportion of GDP in the period 1970 to 1986, and France, where only a slight decline was discernible, the public investment ratio fell sharply. This cannot be attributed to saturation effects. It has been closely associated with attempts to keep government budgets in check — witness the slumps in real public investment in the Community in the periods 1975-78 (− 10.2 per cent) and 1980-84 (− 5.3 per cent).

In their Joint Statement on the Commission's Annual Economic Report 1986-87, the European Trade Unions (ETUC) and the European employers' organizations, UNICE and CEEP, made the following comment on the subject of public investment:[14]

"Public investment and infrastructure investment have suffered under the process of budgetary consolidation, and there is at present some leeway to be made up here. Stronger

> expansion of such investment will make an important contri-
> bution, on both the supply and the demand sides, to achieving
> higher and sustained growth. Such investment should be
> regarded not as a way of compensating for the lack of private
> investment, but as complementary investment undertaken in
> the general interest.''

At the national level, too, support is growing for higher public investment. In 1987, for example, Heinrich Franke, President of the Federal Labour Office in West Germany, called for a ten-year programme of extra public investment in Germany that would cost DM 10,000 million a year.

Opportunities for infrastructure investment are found at the national level as well as at the European level. Many of the investments listed here, while they may need to be initiated by governments, could be financed in whole or in part by private capital or the costs could be recouped through user charges. We return to financing methods in a later section.

The following sectors of infrastructure urgently need more investments:

(a) *Environmental protection.* Success in protecting the environment is essential for a sustainable growth strategy. The next section is devoted to this vital issue.

(b) *Energy saving.* This is an important way to pro-tect the environment since all power plants of whatever kind cause environmental problems. The conservation of energy through combined heat and power schemes, extension of district heating schemes and thermal insulation pro-grammes would generate employment; so would the replacement of non-renewable energy sources (coal, oil, nuclear energy) by renewable sources (sun, wind, water, ambient heat).

(c) *Urban and village renewal.* This includes re-development projects, the rehabilitation of large residential buildings, traffic improvements, and the reclamation and development of industrial sites. New housing, especially for young people, is urgently needed in many cities. Vandalism and petty crime are more prevalent in areas with old dilapidated buildings. Repairing rundown buildings and improving these city districts would be in everyone's interest. The Docklands in London are a good example of this.

(d) *Telecommunications.* Improving the "transport of information" is a major challenge, particularly in southern Europe. In general, Europe needs fewer new highways than in the past, but more "data-highways". Producer service industries have an urgent need for an efficient telecommunications network. It is estimated that in the year 2000 the telecommunications sector will be nearly five times as large as today, amounting to about 7 per cent of GDP.

(e) *Transport.* There are still a number of transport links missing in Europe (the Chunnel is only one) and there is a lack of adequate infrastructure in southern Europe. Conflicts between economic and ecological needs will have to be resolved. Investment in the railway network is necessary to make trains faster and safer and to reduce countries' dependence on oil-using motor traffic. Faster trains will also raise the quality of life for commuters and ease overcrowding in large cities. In many European cities there is a severe shortage of parking spaces, so that cars parking on the street hold up traffic. Adequate parking facilities should be combined with improved inner-city transport to reduce private vehicle use.

(f) *Human services.* Projects capable of creating a great deal of employment in the health sector, in social services, in education and culture can be carried out with comparatively little investment. (A separate section is devoted to culture and education.) The foreseeable rise in the proportion of old people will lead to a greater demand for old-age care. We must organize society better to meet demand for human services. New technologies will require new qualifications. Opportunities for further education of adults must be improved. Better retraining opportunities are preferable to subsidizing jobs which are doomed in the long run. In many countries, there is a great need for improvement of schools.

The European dimension

Completing the European internal market calls for a substantial increase in public investment in the less-favoured countries and regions in order to attract more private investment and accelerate the catching-up process. This is extremely important for economic and social cohesion in the Community and in the whole of Western Europe.

The following European mega-projects are under discussion:

— establishment of a cross-border telecommunications network (costing some 3000 million ECU);
— three combined road/rail/inland waterway networks (costing between 20,000 and 25,000 million ECU);
— the Paris-Brussels-Cologne high-speed rail link (costing 3000 million ECU); and
— the Channel tunnel (costing 4000 million ECU).

Other projects include road links with the Scandinavian countries via Denmark and the Baltic Straits, transalpine rail links through Switzerland and Austria, tidal power plants on the River Severn, the Messina Straits bridge, and the linking up of the Greek, Spanish and Portuguese motorway and rail networks to the main European network. Environmental projects include pollution prevention along the Rhine and clean-up programmes for the Mediterranean, the North Sea and the Baltic Sea.

Infrastructure investment is also urgently needed for a revival of decaying regions with ailing industries, without which it may not be possible to stimulate new enterprises in these areas or prevent long-run decay.

We share the European Commission's view that some countries such as West Germany, Britain and France have succeeded in reducing budget deficits sufficiently to regain room for manoeuvre in fiscal policy. This room for manoeuvre should be used for public investment in "physical and human" infrastructure on a national as well as European scale.

Other countries have budget deficits that are so large that the interest burden on public debt does not give them much room for expansion. Interest rates too tend to be very high. Interest rate subsidies for important projects or a more relaxed monetary policy would help to improve the profitability of investment. If inflation in these countries were tackled by moderate nominal wage increases, there would also be more scope for an accommodating monetary policy.

Generally speaking, countries that have aleady attained high living standards are more concerned with improving the quality of life, whereas in others generating higher incomes may be given priority. Among the suggested investment projects, investment in traditional infrastructure (in particular, telecommunications) will be more important in the South, environment protection and urban renewal in the North—although the need for environmental protection in the South is just as great or even greater.

3. Job creation through environmental protection

"Environmental protection will be as important in the next decade as national defence now." (Bruno Kreisky, at the first Vienna meeting of the Commission)

"Environmental technologies will be more important than Star Wars technologies." (Amit Bhaduri, at the first Vienna meeting of the Commission)

The sense of helplessness that followed publication of the Club of Rome report in 1974 contributed to a prevailing growth pessimism. To overcome this pessimism we need to show how economic growth and environmental sensitivity can be reconciled. Growth has to be twisted or moulded towards environmental protection and skill-enhancing production methods. This is also one of the conclusions of the Brundtland Report. Economic growth does not necessarily mean more pollution and more concrete blocks blighting the landscape.

The idea popularized in the 1970s that zero growth is necessary to protect the environment is, in our view, wholly misconceived. We are in strong agreement with the conclusions of the Brundtland Commission that poverty and misery are the greatest enemies of environmental protection and that environmental problems can only be solved by higher growth rates to generate the necessary resources.

These problems cannot be solved by market mechanisms any more than can the provision of national defence. Pollution control is a task to be tackled by society as a whole, because individual and voluntary actions can be negated by the behaviour of others and because people can gain the benefits without paying (the "free rider" problem). It is best financed through "compulsory levies", which may take the form of higher taxes (for example, on leaded petrol) or of mandatory measures involving higher production costs and hence higher prices (such as the requirement for new cars to be equipped with catalytic converters). Pollution control is basically a responsibility of the State, acting for its increasingly environmentally conscious citizens and their descendants.

Environmental policy is mainly an attempt to influence economic development so as to manage the flow of waste residuals and pollutants and reduce damaging side-effects of production and consumption such as soil erosion and the cutting of tropical forests. Management of the environment thus attempts to alleviate air and water pollution, regulate the use and disposal of toxic substances, manage the disposal of solid wastes, and enhance the safety of the workplace. Safety and health at work are an integral part of the human environment.

A large amount of resources will be required to remedy accumulated environmental damage and prevent further ecological harm. If the problems of environment are taken seriously, as much money may have to be invested in environmental protection by the end of the century as is currently being invested in armaments. People have been convinced of the necessity to spend many billions on armaments; they should also be persuadable that huge sums are needed for ecological purposes. The purpose is the same: to defend their and their descendants' future existence.

Much money is now spent, and donated by individuals, on clearing up after environmental accidents and helping their victims, or on trying to restitute damage already done. How much better it would have been if this money had been spent in advance.

During the last few years, in particular, there have been a number of environmental catastrophes:

— the nuclear power station incident at Chernobyl;
— the leakage in the pesticide plant in Bhopal, India, which resulted in 2000 fatalities and more than 200,000 injured;
— the contamination of the Rhine in the wake of the fire at a chemical warehouse owned by Sandoz, and other chemical spills; and
— the poisonous algoid blooming and the seal deaths in the North Sea.

Far more alarming, however, is the slow and undramatic deterioration of the conditions of human life, which ultimately may make the globe uninhabitable—the reduction of the ozone layer, the increased concentration of carbon dioxide and nitrogen oxides in the atmosphere, and the slow but steady poisoning of the earth and air with toxic chemicals such as dioxin and heavy metals. Much needs to be done—to cut acid rain "fall-out" from burning fossil fuels, curb vehicle exhaust pollutants, replant forests, halt soil erosion, and so on. All these tasks will create additional jobs.

It has been said that the "spillover effects" of armament expenditures are conducive to technological progress and thus of general benefit to the population. This same reasoning should be applied to expenditure on environmental protection, which also has vast technological potential.

Environmental protection offers a wide range of investment possibilities that are comparable to the investment needs of the welfare state. Environmental investments may meet with greater popular support, since the risks of an environmental disaster are more evenly distributed among the population.

Environmental protection primarily calls for the following measures:

— repair of existing environmental damage;
— waste management by additional filters, wastewater purification plants, recycling programmes and noise reduction measures;
— prevention of damage through ecologically beneficial technology (including in agriculture);
— improving the working environment.

For the long term, prevention is the most important. Environmental policies should therefore be closely tied to policies on technology and innovation. Environmental protection is also a key component of preventive health care.

Indispensable environmental investments

> "We must not die poisoned while politicians quarrel over who will pay the bill." (Clas-Erik Odhner, at the second Vienna meeting of the Commission)

Public spending on the environment in OECD countries currently average between 1 per cent and $1\frac{1}{2}$ per cent of GDP. The main item in the bill is water treatment, accounting for about one-half of total costs. Waste collection represents about one-quarter of the total.

High expenditure in the near future will be necessary to prevent cumulative environmental damage, especially in southern Europe, which spends less than 0.5 per cent of GDP in this area. Europe as a whole will need to double its current spending to nearly 3 per cent of GDP (on the restrictive definition of the OECD). However, the OECD definition relates only to spending on severe environmental pollution. It should be practicable to establish a broader definition of environmental spending which includes the following:

— preventive measures: a more efficient use of energy and raw materials, avoiding the use of highly toxic materials as inputs and their generation as waste matter; and

— measures aimed at creating more humane environmental conditions: the reduction of noise levels and traffic in residential areas, protection of the countryside, and so on.

On this wider definition, expenditure on environmental protection would need to amount to as least 4 per cent of GDP by 1990, which would create additional employment if the financing is at least partly additional.

The report *Challenge for Europe*, by the Nordic and West German trade unions,[15] lists the main tasks of pollution control for several European countries:

"In Denmark, excessive use of fertilizers leads to a permanent pollution of drinking water. Efforts in the field should be aimed at reducing the use of fertillizers and improving purification plants. In Great Britain, water supplies are threatened by outdated sewerage systems. Renewal of these systems would create a considerable number of jobs. A common task of Mediterranean countries and countries surrounding the North and the Baltic Sea is cleaning up these waters by means of improved pollution control. Hence all rivers flowing into them must in the future be less polluted and at the same time the dumping of poison and other chemical garbage into the sea must be prohibited. As to the Baltic Sea, there is a difficult collaboration with Eastern European countries, which should be facilitated by a programme for technical and financial cooperation for environment. A common European pollution problem is the so-called 'forest death', the result of serious air pollution."

The profitability of European enterprises has improved in recent years and they are now better able to cope with regulations requiring investment in pollution control. Joint European efforts can ensure that this is achieved without detriment to competitiveness.

The working environment

> "Environmental protection starts at the work place."
> (Stephen Pursey, at the Helsinki meeting of the Commission)

> "Claims for a 'social codex' (minimum regulations for
> employment) are being rejected by less developed countries
> which regard this as a kind of protectionism." (Francis Blan-
> chard, Director General of ILO, at the Paris meeting of the
> Commission)

Prevention of damage to the environment and the health
of the population is directly related to improvements in
the protection of the health and safety of workers. They
are the citizens in the front line of the drive for cleaner,
safer methods of production. Furthermore, enormous
social and economic costs are currently incurred by
individuals, enterprises and public social security and
health care systems in remedying the damage resulting
from unsafe working conditions.

A European-wide effort to invest in improved occupational health and safety standards would yield major
returns in the form of reductions in time off work for
sickness and ill-health, increased productivity, lower
social security pay-outs and reduced pressure on health
care systems. In addition, cleaner, safer workplaces also
reduce the potential for leakages of environmentally
damaging products into the community as a whole. In
terms of employment creation this would require more
people to research and apply safe technologies and working practices and enhanced inspection systems to enforce
tougher regulations. However, it is quite probable that in
net terms resources would be released from those currently applied to clean up the aftermath of unsafe and
unclean working practices and treat its victims.

In the increasingly unified European market of the 1990s it is essential that improved regulation be applied to avoid the danger of unfair competition between "dirty" countries and those operating to the highest standards. We must avoid the possibility of jobs being transferred from countries applying responsible environmental policies to those lagging behind. There is now a major effort to extend the "Seveso" Directive on major hazards of the European Community led by the international trade union movement. This could be a model for a European and indeed world-wide campaign for international standards on environmental protection.

Improving occupational health and safety is best achieved with the close involvement of trade union representatives trained in the application of the relevant regulations. While state-authorized inspectors will always be needed, they must be backed up by agreed systems established between unions and employers at the workplace. Governmental backing for improved occupational health and safety is however essential both to prevent "free riders" avoiding their social obligations and to ensure a practical co-operation between those employed in potentially environmentally damaging industries and the community as a whole.

Employment effects

"Without investment in environmental protection, civil engineering would be heading for a crisis." (Karl-Georg Zinn, at the second Vienna meeting of the Commission)

The positive effects of environmental protection on employment may be expected chiefly through the additional economic growth that could be generated. If environmental policies result in an increase in investment and production, this will in turn provide additional employment. There can be no doubt that environmental protection would have a favourable effect on employment, notwithstanding possible negative consequences such as an increase in costs, reduced investment in the construction of power stations, and so on. Nevertheless, there could initially be a lowering of living standards as conventionally measured since we now have to pay for the sins of the past.

Employment effects will depend not only on the amount of growth generated but on the type of growth brought about by pollution control measures. As a result of changes induced by environmental policies, production is likely to become more labour-intensive. Consequently, extra employment will be generated, even if the overall rate of growth remains unchanged. The increase in labour intensity may be direct, due, for example, to pollution control technologies that require a relatively high labour input, or indirect, when it is the consequence of higher prices for polluting products such as a shift in demand towards services that are less polluting (and more labour-intensive) than industrial production.

Where would the jobs come from? The "public works" aspect of environmental protection is an essential feature. For example, pulling down buildings spoiling the Mediterranean coast, constructing new parks, cleaning the beaches every day, and so on, would provide as many jobs as a more conventional programme of public works.

In the majority of cases pollution control currently involves extra expenditure. This will always be true of remedial work. But in the medium and long term it should be possible to streamline pollution control expenditures to some extent, so that extra costs may decrease.

Regulations requiring pollution control tend to create jobs in the construction sector, in those industries that manufacture, operate, maintain and service pollution control equipment, in public services and in the administrative sector (drafting, implementing, monitoring and enforcing the regulations).

There is a growing appreciation of the contribution of environmental policies to job creation. In recent years a number of EC countries have introduced job creation schemes directly connected with the protection of the environment.[16] Three programmes in Denmark provided a total of about 11,000 new jobs between 1975 and 1983. In France, for every job directly created in water purification activities and noise abatement measures, three to four jobs were generated in associated sectors. In West Germany, an estimated 380,000 new jobs were generated by public and private spending on pollution control, and in the Netherlands some 70,000 jobs were created in 1982 as a result of environmental programmes. All these figures exclude the multiplier effect on other sectors of the economy.

It is estimated that in waste disposal and treatment alone between 50,000 and 120,000 jobs will be created in the European Community by 1995.

In West Germany, the IFO Institute estimated that as many as 200,000 new jobs could be created by proposals from the Social Democratic Party on employment and environment.[17] About half the additional investment would be offset by higher tax yields. A one billion DM programme for environmental protection would create about 14,000 jobs. According to estimates from the Umweltbundesamt Berlin, the costs of remedial measures alone could amount to at least 17 billion DM. However, many German cities have had to postpone urgent environmental investment (particularly repair of sewerage systems) because of budgetary constraints. Financial help from central government would be essential.

The impact on employment in any particular country will vary depending upon the extent to which demands for materials and equipment to combat pollution can be met from domestic markets.

If an environmental protection programme were carried out in all European countries, the additional spending would have a multiplier effect of 1.5 to 2—that is, the value added would be 1.5 to 2 times the original expenditures. This, in turn, would affect employment, particularly in the labour-intensive construction sector.

Environmental regulations not only create jobs but can save jobs in tourism, agriculture, outdoor recreation and all other sectors which depend on preservation of baseline ecosystems.

The European Commission has suggested a programme of demonstration projects over five years to explore the job-creating possibilities of environmental policies, but funds for the programme have not yet been forthcoming.

At the present time the main concern is with remedying previous damage. However, less costly preventive measures are gaining in importance. The impact on employment from remedial measures is normally greater because they are less likely to involve rationalization. If, for instance, an existing power station has to be updated with a fume-desulphurization unit, this invariably leads to relatively high additional investment and operating costs.

In general, pollution control regulations involve investments which are to some extent additional to "normal" capital investments. In addition, once pollution equipment is installed, it often requires extra manpower for its operation and maintenance.

Pollution control may lead to higher prices for certain products. But these higher prices reflect changes in the nature and quality of the product and are thus not comparable with "normal" inflation. For example, the purchaser of a car with a catalytic converter is buying a car plus a certain amount of cleaner air. In other words, the cost of a car includes a charge for air pollution which was previously ignored.

"Smokestack" industries are particularly hit by environmental regulations. Arguments that their competitiveness is thereby impaired are misplaced; Japan and the United States have more severe regulations. But environmental policy in Europe needs to be co-ordinated to prevent industries shifting their locations from one country to another to avoid controls. For individual countries to attract industry by lax regulations for polluters would be a disastrous strategy.

To prevent further ecological damage, even tighter controls on new equipment are necessary. Much more investment is needed in new technology to prevent pollution, which offers big opportunities to boost employment. Interestingly from the viewpoint of educational planning, environmental policies largely involve interdisciplinary work.

Environmental protection is a social task. Since it is

unchecked technological development that is responsible for environmental problems, a solution cannot be based on free enterprise. Those causing pollution are not faced with the costs it imposes, which are external and often widely spread. Moreover, accumulated damage may be recognizable only at a much later stage.

Government plays a decisive role in environmental protection through public investment (such as disposal of wastes) as well as by laying down regulations and offering financial assistance to companies. However the problems are handled, the solutions will contribute considerably towards creating new jobs. Much as the construction of the railway system at one time greatly stimulated economic development, so too will environmental protection and related technologies.

4. Technology and innovation policy

"Many of our important technologies would not exist without public incentive." (Bruno Kreisky, at the second Vienna meeting of the Commission)

"Innovation—not wages—is the main weapon of competition in highly industrialized societies." (Ewald Walterskirchen, at the second Vienna meeting of the Commission)

New technologies do not create jobs in the same way as, for example, new infrastructure. Their introduction is nevertheless essential for a successful economy that can support full employment. There is a widespread misconception that rationalization and automation are important reasons for the rise in unemployment. Microelectronics, in particular, is considered to be a job-killer.

However, the positive effects of technical progress, though less obvious, outweigh the negative ones. Technical progress needs much labour input (research and development, production of new machines, and so on) and generates additional income through higher productivity which is spent on goods and services. A highly industrialized country that does not continuously develop new technologies is bound to decline and to lose export market shares.

One of the lessons from Japan's experience is that rapid technological development can lead to low unemployment.

Those manufacturing industries with the highest productivity growth also have the strongest rise in employment. On balance, new technologies are employment-creating in advanced economies because they increase investment, create new markets and improve competitiveness. Europe's industry can only compete by fostering technology and innovation. Promoting this kind of industrial adjustment is a major challenge, in which governments have an active role to play.

Innovation policy has become a major issue in economic debate. In the past, policies to stimulate investment and innovation have focused on physical investment such as machinery. This approach helps capital-intensive industries but neglects those where physical investment is of secondary importance, including the high-tech and engineering sectors which are crucial for future growth. These industries may have to spend years developing new products and processes before they can profitably sell them on the market.

The stimulation of innovation requires encouragement for research and development, including subsidies or credit guarantees. In industry, development accounts for the lion's share of R & D spending, sometimes up to 90 per cent of total costs.

Governments help finance research and development in the United States and elsewhere. In West Germany, R & D in private industry is partly financed by the Ministry of Technology. However, large companies receive the most funding. Help should increasingly be extended to small and medium-sized firms which cannot carry out the necessary R & D without assistance. The government's share in financing could be combined with a share in subsequent profits.

Structural adjustment policies must embrace both innovative and old established industries. One reason for high unemployment is that governments (and both sides of industry) tend to care more about preserving existing jobs than creating new ones. However, the deterioration of the employment situation has been due more to a slowdown in new job openings than a loss of old jobs. Two-thirds of the EC's budget goes on subsidizing agriculture, a sector representing 3 per cent of value added. The much-vaunted ESPRIT programme, which is supposed to launch Europe into new technologies on the same footing as Japan, has a budget equal to the subsidy on sugar beet.

Key aims of industrial policy are to boost employment and enhance a country's position in the world economic hierarchy. Most European nations also want to maintain high real wages. This can be achieved only by producing goods and developing production methods that cannot be copied easily, which means a constant process of technological innovation to keep abreast and ahead of the market.

After the war, Europe went through a period of technical imitation. In many areas it has now caught up with the United States. But all too often research and innovation are not translated into commercial success.

Technology policy should try to achieve complementary developments in different industries and services. Co-ordination is essential.

An atmosphere of innovation must be created. Most new developments are born within existing companies. The clearest sign that economic policy takes technology and innovation seriously is to provide funds for R & D.

One of the tasks of technology policy is to improve contacts between firms and universities. Another is to make it easier for innovative entrepreneurs to start new small enterprises or expand existing ones through venture capital and so on.

It is essential that technical innovation is linked to market success. Market success is more likely to be achieved if the State is not only subsidizing R & D but also buying the product. This applies, for example, to environmental protection technologies and telecommunications. As with armaments, research is then being promoted by institutions that have an interest in their success.

There is another reason why government stimulus is needed for technological and scientific development. Free enterprise expects quick results. Scientific and technological development, however, rarely provides them.

A greater role for human skills in technology

For many people, industrial society is synonymous with assembly lines, mass production and giant corporations.

However, the development of technologies and their applications are not independent of cultures and societies. There is scope for deliberate attempts to build into new technological developments a greater role for human skills. Volvo is a good example of this.

Throughout the nineteenth century, two strands of technological development were in collision. One was craft production, founded on the idea that machines and processes could augment the craftsman's skills. The other was mass production, based on decomposing each task into single steps capable of being performed by machines. "The visionaries of craft production foresaw a world of small producers, each specialized in one line of work and dependent on the others. The visionaries of mass production foresaw a world of ever more automated factories, run by ever fewer and ever less skilled workers."[18]

The victory of mass production methods seemed complete. Recently, however, mass production has begun to run into trouble; the advantages of economies of scale have not always outweighed the disadvantages of large bureaucratic organizations.

At the same time, there has been an impressive resurgence of much more flexible and specialized small enterprises in manufacturing and in producer services.

The devaluation of labour skills through mass production is increasingly seen as a disastrous mistake. The efficiency of robot factories is much lower than expected. Japanese studies show that the production time lost through computer failures and reprogramming robots has been grossly underestimated.

The influence of governments on technological development may not be decisive, but as far as there are options, the high-skill variant should be chosen—another example of "twisting" the nature of growth.

5. Culture and education

"Culture is becoming more and more important in local government politics." (Hilmar Hoffmann, at the second Vienna meeting of the Commission)

According to the famous article by C.P. Snow, there are two types of intelligence and culture—a literary-humanistic one and a technical-scientific one. The eternal dream of integrating the "two cultures" raises hopes for a technologically advanced and culturally rich society.

In order for culture (in the narrow sense as "humanistic" culture) to be enjoyed, it must have been first absorbed through education, and people must have the leisure and incomes to do so. Even in the richer countries of Europe only about one-fifth of the population has the appropriate education fully to appreciate culture.

Culture and technology are closely related to education. An expansion of education (including adult education) would—besides generating a large demand for teaching jobs—create the more educated producers that the new technologies require and the more educated "absorbers of culture". There is also a need for qualitative educational reform that might well require more teachers.

Moreover, culture has always been a dynamic, spontaneous and critical element in society. Always receptive to the new, it is a kind of model for technological innovation. For this reason, education needs to encourage not only functional skills but also extrafunctional ones, such as imagination and experimentation—particularly via the arts. Thus Lother Späth, Prime Minister of the state of Baden-Württemberg and a leading German advocate of technology policy, has recently called for the promotion of creative and artistic development.

The historian Jacob Burckhardt distinguished culture from religion and state by its attributes of freedom, spontaneity and mobility. There are signs that humanistic culture and technological sciences—representing the inner and the outer world, personality and reality—are gaining ground in European society. This growing interest should be promoted. Cultural needs are virtually without limit, in practice "insatiable".

Culture includes education as well as the arts. In both areas unemployment and precarious employment have been on the increase. Many teachers, artists and musicians cannot find work after completing their education or must accept jobs that do not match their skills.

Meanwhile, there is growing need for their services. The demand for adult education and retraining is not being satisfied in many countries at a time when rapid structural changes in the economy make retraining all the more necessary. For the long-term unemployed, retraining may be the only way back to work. New institutional arrangements are needed to co-ordinate life-long and basic education.

There is also a lack of kindergarten facilities (with suitable time schedules for working parents), and of all-day schools in many European countries. As far as theatre, music and the visual arts are concerned, cultural needs are not being satisfied outside city areas.

This section deals with an aspect of the unemployment problem which, while not as significant quantitatively as some other aspects, is of political relevance. A substantial amount of unemployment, in the field of culture particularly, affects young people who have just finished school or higher education.

Jobs in cultural activities

"There is a wide range of cultural activities where employment could expand. What we need is a symbiosis of private and public cultural promotion." (Hilmar Hoffmann, at the Mallorca meeting of the Commission)

We are concerned here not only with "high culture", but also with commercialized culture, with leisure activities and with the alternative cultural scene.

As with infrastructure and environmental investment, the promotion of culture depends on a symbiosis of public and private sectors. Subsidies for cultural activities are legitimated by their external effects. Culture is increasingly a factor in location decisions and is now seen a key determinant of the image of an area. It acts as a magnet to attract visitors, investors and highly qualified personnel. In the core of Europe, traditional location factors are losing significance. Conventional infrastructure within each country has become more uniform. Culture, however, is a source of differentiation. Some European cities now consider their cultural policy as part of economic promotion. Studies of public spending on culture demonstrate a high multiplier effect through encouragement of substantial additional private expenditure.

In the course of economic development, more and more people acquire standard material goods, such as telephones and washing machines, and demand for these tends to level off as income rises. Instead, people look increasingly for products which display their individuality or status, such as antiques or winter holidays in the sun. They also demand more culture—the supply of which, unlike that of antiques or tropical beaches, can be expanded without limit. "Culture—the new growth industry" was the title of an article in the German weekly magazine, *Die Zeit*. One of the fastest growing industries in Europe today is—funnily enough—museums. All countries are building museums of various kinds, including industrial and open-air museums, to feed people's curiosity about roots and origins. Summer arts festivals are fully booked and "cultural tourism" is booming. Fulfilling people's cultural demands is a way of encouraging spending, which generates jobs. However, culture is far more than consumption. Culture means to create music, literature and art. Culture is continuous and critical intellectual searching.

In his book *Culture for Tomorrow*,[19] Hilmar Hoffmann describes various ways of creating new jobs in cultural activities. The growing book, music and video market, for instance, has great potential for employment. A reduction of working hours would augment the possibilities offered. In order to expand cultural opportunities and programmes an appropriate material and personnel infrastructure is necessary: district libraries, adult evening classes, lecture halls, museums. The city of Frankfurt may be considered a model example, with cultural spending accounting for 11 per cent of the city's entire budget. Culture there has become one of the most important local political issues.

The music market is expanding rapidly. The annual turnover in West Germany amounts to more than 25 billion DM, providing jobs for 230,000 people. There is a symbiosis of the public and private domain. The more music schools there are, the more teachers will find employment which in turn helps boost the production of the musical instrument and record industry. Even publicity is concerned with art and culture since it offers employment to creative people. An ever-growing number of jobs are being created in newspapers, television (including satellite broadcasting) and the video, book and art markets.

There is also great scope for increasing employment in leisure industries: sports, gymnastics, leisure parks, and so on. Investments in leisure parks in France are expected to create about 85,000 jobs in depressed areas over four years.

There is a close relation between culture and design. In this respect, Europe with its great cultural and artistic tradition has an advantage. Italian products have a world reputation for good looks and innovative design. Finland, too, is famous for design. Finally, the close relation between leisure and culture should not be overlooked. Quite a number of sociologists believe that our societies will shift somewhat from a work-and-money orientation to a leisure orientation. With a gradual reduction in working hours and longer holidays, cultural and educational needs will have room to develop fully.

In sum, in a strategy to fight unemployment, culture plays a dual role. First, it is a very labour-intensive sector—this is particularly true for cultural institutions. And second, private cultural expenditures are rising faster than income. Thus satisfying cultural needs becomes increasingly important with rising levels of income.

There needs to be a broad eclectic promotion of cultural initiatives and institutions, with much more decentralization. Limited public funds necessitate more private sponsors of culture.

Education

"Education in Europe has become too rigid at all levels." (Kari Kairamo, at the Helsinki meeting of the Commission)

Unemployment of well-educated people means that a large investment in education is wasted. Nowadays there is no educational level that can provide full protection from unemployment. In West Germany the rate of unemployment among skilled workers has quadrupled during the first half of the 1980s, while that for engineers and medical doctors has tripled. During that period approximately one-third of the population were personally affected by unemployment. Unemployment rates of high school and university graduates are still much lower than average, but they are rising. Moreover, the well educated often do not find jobs commensurate with their qualifications.

Surveys throughout Europe show that people want more education, training and retraining after they have left school. The majority are less interested in vocational training than in more general education to "make them more whole". The educational needs of adults are not being satisfied at present.

Economic restructuring requires continuous education and learning. On average, an employee holds three different jobs over his working life. Greater flexibility of manpower requires constantly increasing knowledge and expertise. In particular, technical knowledge and research plays a crucial role. The key to competitiveness lies in the general standard of education and the quantity and quality of technological resources.

This is an area where Western Europe has lagged behind. The European Commission and European industry have expressed concern over the state of education in Europe. Whereas well over half of American school children and three-quarters of Japanese go on to tertiary level studies, the corresponding proportion in Europe is only 15–35 per cent. Of course, people will only invest time and money in education and training if they can expect to find an adequate job thereafter.

Only one European in 10,000 has taken a postgraduate degree, compared to one in 1000 Americans who have PhDs. The low esteem accorded to technical subjects in Europe is reflected in the fact that only one postgraduate student in five chooses technological or natural science subjects. In Japan one in five opt for the technology sector alone, which may help explain Japan's ability constantly to launch new products on the market.

The education sector has to operate in a fast-moving world. What is needed is a system capable of rapidly responding to the demands of an information society and sufficiently flexible in structure to facilitate constant updating and enable every individual to go on learning throughout life.

Education should provide soundly-based broad qualifications that enable people to adjust to changes. Educational opportunities for adults must be developed, including the right for employees to take educational leave. Education for young people requires major structural changes, with a shift of emphasis from discipline and memorizing details to a more creative and thematic approach based on understanding. It would go beyond the scope of our report to discuss these changes in detail. We just want to stress that the high youth unemployment in many countries apparently has a close connection to deficient and obsolete traditional school systems. Training and retraining are dealt with at more length in the section on labour market policy.

6. New jobs in information services

"Services do not need subsidies, but a policy friendly to services." (Günther Pauli, at the Mallorca meeting of the Commission)

"Central Europe is lagging behind in human services." (Hans-Jürgen Krupp, at the second Vienna meeting of the Commission)

There has been a marked long-term shift of employment from manufacturing to services. Between 1963 and 1983, employment in services rose in Europe by 19 million, while industry and agriculture lost 16 million jobs. Economic policy, on the other hand, has tended to neglect services and is still tailored to the needs of industry.

More than half the European labour force now works in the service sector. The highest figure is 68 per cent for the Netherlands and Belgium. Europe dominates world trade in services—with France taking a clear lead over the UK. Now, Europe is facing a major assault on several traditional service sectors, including banking, insurance, and transport where the Japanese are building up a "second wave".

Europe has a clear potential advantage in linguistic services, design, and cultural industries, to name a few. The service sector is very heterogeneous, but can be split into three main areas— producer services, public services and private services for households. Producer services are intermediate services to other producers. This fast-growing field (software, databanks, and so on) offers the best hope for more employment in the service sector. However, the development of producer services is closely tied to the health of industry. Increasingly, producer services (such as software) are also purchased by private households.

The real consumption of services to private households has not been rising as a proportion of total household expenditure as many people imagine. The proportion of household income spent on services has increased because they have become more expensive owing to smaller productivity gains.

In some European countries, almost one-half of employees in the service sector are working in public administration, health and education.

Employment in the public sector grew rapidly in the postwar decades, but since 1984 expansion has ceased in many countries. Public services, such as health and education, are very labour-intensive. They have shown low or unmeasurable increases in productivity and so have become continuously more expensive in relation to goods. The rising relative cost of public services has been reflected in higher taxes. This has been a key factor in the "crisis of the welfare state". People have seen little visible improvement in the provision of public services, which has reinforced resistance to higher taxes.

The need for high quality public services is by no

means satisfied. But the public sector will probably not be able to expand in future as it did in the past. Prospects for jobs in services, including high-skill jobs, rest with the private sector.

It is important to realize that employment in services need not mean low-skill, low-wage jobs. In the United States, often held up as a model, inadequate welfare benefits and an influx of poorly educated workers to the labour force have resulted in rapid expansion of low-paid jobs in low-productivity services.

In Europe, high minimum wages and non-wage labour costs, coupled with more generous unemployment insurance, have discouraged a similar trend. While this has resulted in more open unemployment in conditions of slow economic growth, it also gives Europe an opportunity to choose a different route to jobs based on a high-skill, high-wage economy, in which information services can play an important part.

The expansion of information services

"One of the biggest single cultural changes in Europe is the arrival of the new communications technologies." (Richard Hoggart, at the London meeting of the Commission)

New services are a dynamic force of the European economy. There are a number of double-digit growth sectors in services, the majority of them information or communication services. These include linguistic services, courier services, software development and computer-related services, business communication, mobile communications, design, leisure and entertainment. The single most important barrier to trade is the language barrier. The linguistic communications market is therefore growing rapidly. Courier and express parcel services are also a fast expanding market. Speedy delivery of packages and documents saves much time and warehouse space. There is, however, a need to unify postal and customs regulations. Some customs authorities are not willing to allow 24-hour clearance even if all costs for overtime are paid.

New information technologies have resulted in large productivity gains in several service industries. Some people have called this "the industrialization of services". However, the success stories of new service companies feature very rarely in the media compared with the closing of factories and consequent redundancies.

Services cannot flourish without industry, but industry cannot compete without services. If industry wishes to improve its competitiveness it needs to put some resources into boosting the efficiency of services. In the new service companies the largest cost is people. The second largest cost is communications and computers. Thus telecommunications and information policies are of strategic importance.

Today, only 8 per cent of services are internationally traded, compared to 45 per cent of industrial output. France is the world's second largest exporter of services after the United States. The biggest new competitor is, once again, Japan.

New service industries can argue, rightly, that manufacturing industry did not have to invest in roads, railways, harbours and power stations. These were normally provided by governments which accepted that they were a necessary precondition for economic development.

Service companies, too, should have flexible and cost-efficient access to computers and communications just as manufacturing industries buy energy. Governments have provided industry with the necessary infrastructure. What the new service sector needs is an efficient and cheap telecommunications network. In many European countries, public telecommunication services are subsidizing public postal services. This, of course, raises call charges. PTTs need to master the computer technologies which converge with the telecom networks. As long as a telephone call from Brussels to Geneva is as expensive as one from New York to Geneva, some European countries will suffer a comparative disadvantage in business at home and abroad. Obstacles such as incompatible communications systems within Europe must also be overcome.

New producer services have to survive largely without economic policy incentives. For example, in most European countries, tax authorities do not accept depreciation schemes which involve writing off assets over as little as two years.

Large enterprises have invested heavily in personnel, computer and communication facilities. Smaller companies and start-ups do not have the financial strength to do the same, nor can they build up their own databanks. New services in the areas of information-processing are preparing the ground for entrepreneurship. The new self-employed have little capital, but considerable skills and motivation. The main investment in a new service business—apart from a computer—is manpower. Software industries offer jobs particularly for young people. The average age of a software programmer is 21 years. Many of them have no appropriate formal education but have turned a hobby into a business. For information workers, creativity and imagination are as important as formal qualifications. The biggest obstacle to growth in information-processing services is adequate human resources.

Part IV: International Opportunities

1. Prospects for East-West co-operation

"Since medieval times, the political situation in Europe has been characterized by permanent conflicts. Now, we have a chance." (Karl Georg Zin, at the second Vienna meeting of the Commission)

So far we have concentrated mainly on West European problems and solutions within the context of West European economies and institutions. However, Europe has another, poorer, Eastern half that cannot be ignored, either politically or economically.

The benefits of increased political co-operation between East and West are obvious. We all applaud recent successes in the arms control negotiations. Thus we would only emphasize the obvious point that military and political détente between the superpowers could have a positive effect on prospects for increased East-West co-operation in less political areas such as trade and the protection of the environment.

The environment

One area where East-West co-operation could bring concrete results is in controlling environmental pollution. Pollution is an international problem: acid rain, radioactive fallout, ozone-destroying chemicals, recognize no boundaries and pay no customs duties. The need for clear-cut, prompt and, above all, co-ordinated action is growing more pressing by the day. Since the countries of East and West Europe share one European "sub-ecosystem", it is imperative that they act together against pollution.

It is probably true to say that the higher a country's living standards, the greater public concern for the environment, and the more open the society, the more pressure can be brought to bear on government. Thus while public and official recognition of pollution as a serious problem is relatively recent in Western Europe, it is even more recent in Eastern Europe. Most of these countries' governments, with the notable exception of Romania, have begun to address the issue and some have set aside funds for cleaning up the environment. But their efforts are hopelessly inadequate for the task at hand.

It is impossible to say with certainty that pollution is worse in Eastern Europe than in the West. However, it is extremely serious throughout the region. For instance, pollution from acid rain caused by the burning of lignite has reached alarming proportions in three areas.

One is the golden triangle of Leipzig, Karl Marx Stadt and Dresden in East Germany, a country with the highest emission of sulphur dioxide per head in the world. A second area is the coal mining and steel complex of Katowice/Nova Huta in southern Poland, whose corrosive fumes are responsible for the destruction of one of the country's architectural shrines, the nearby city of Krakow. Finally there is Czechoslovakia's black belt of northern Bohemia where a choking black smog hangs over the hills, killing the trees and ruining the health of those who live there. It is such an unpopular area to live that the government pays the inhabitants an extra 2000 crowns a year as a "stabilizing payment"; the locals call it "burial money".[20]

The emphasis on rapid development of heavy industry in Eastern Europe has led to energy-intensive forms of production. In general, machinery is obsolete and inefficient; managers do not have the needed incentives to conserve energy or to avoid pollution. These problems originate in part from the system of highly centralized planning which has dominated the economies of Eastern Europe since the Second World War.

The CMEA countries are in the throes of a fundamental reappraisal of their economic and political systems as a result of Mikhail Gorbachev's attempts at reform in the Soviet Union. The ideas being debated in the USSR and in some other East European countries could make a difference to how they tackle environmental questions. *Perestroika* is intended to make firms more cost conscious and more efficient. This could lead to cleaner, less energy-intensive factories. *Glasnost*, or the policy of openness, could allow the formation of alternative pressure groups within society.

In this context, what can be done to increase East–West co-operation on the environment?

There has already been some limited progress in this area, mainly under the aegis of the United Nations Economic Commission for Europe. For example, most European countries have agreed to reduce sulphur emission levels by 30 per cent (Romania is again an exception). But progress within the Commission is slow. Here Britain is showing extreme insensitivity for the environmental concerns of its neighbours. When discussing pollution problems with East European countries Western Europe cannot boast that it is simon-pure.

We believe co-operation on environmental matters could be initiated or increased in three key areas:

(a) International agreements on pollution control; a European or international environmental protection agency with on-site monitoring capabilities could be established.

(b) Co-operation on financing, for example through loans or grants, for pollution control in the poorer regions of Europe, including Eastern Europe.

(c) Transfer of "cleaner"technology—which would entail a rationalization of Cocom regulations—to improve the standard of East European industrial production.

(d) The big credits that have recently been offered to the Soviet Union and the Eastern countries by the four big Western European countries should be used also for these purposes.

Trade

Trade between East and West has been growing, with various ups and downs, since the 1960s but has always been much more important for CMEA members than for the West. Trade with Eastern Europe and the Soviet Union accounts for only about 3-4 per cent of total OECD trade, but imports from and exports to the OECD make up from 10 to 35 per cent of individual CMEA countries' trade. Total exports from the CMEA are heavily weighted towards raw materials, mainly oil and gas, from the Soviet Union.

A more prosperous Eastern Europe, which has about 400 million inhabitants, could provide a large market for Western goods, though differences in the economic systems create difficulties that will not be easy to overcome. The obstacles to increasing trade between the two blocs are both political and economic. In some debt-ridden Eastern countries—Poland, Romania and, to a lesser extent, Hungary and Bulgaria—a major problem is shortage of hard currency. The lack of an adequate pricing system is also a serious impediment to trade liberalization.

At the same time, the East European economies seem to have great difficulties in generating long-term growth in hard currency exports. Falling prices for raw materials have led to import cuts across the board in most of the countries.

The recently concluded agreement on mutual recognition between the CMEA and EC offers some hope for future co-operation. The Soviet Union has conceded that the EC may negotiate bilateral agreements with individual CMEA members, which is crucial to the success of negotiations currently underway between the EC and Hungary, Romania, Czechoslovakia and Poland. The USSR and the EC may also begin negotiations in the near future. Depending on the specifics of each agreement, some increase in trade could result. Yugoslavia, which is not a CMEA member, has expressed interest in an arrangement with EFTA.

Western Europe should grasp the opportunity presented by reform plans in the Soviet Union. Eastern Europe has many economic problems that would benefit from Western technologies and expertise, to help modernize industry, improve the distribution system and so on. China has several thousand joint ventures with Western countries, the Soviet Union currently far fewer, though it is keen to attract more.

There is a considerable potential for growth. For example, in East Germany the influence of *glasnost* and *perestroika* may stimulate more joint ventures and investment possibilities, which are now restricted for political reasons. West Germany too curtails technology exports through the Cocom system under which Western nations restrict access to "sensitive" technology by Communist countries. In the long run, there is a legitimate hope for better economic and political relations which could well result in an economic regeneration for both countries.

2. Development assistance

"The economic crisis of the developing countries may be a threat to blossoming democracies just as youth unemployment may be a threat to Western democracies." (Amit Bhaduri, at the Mallorca meeting of the Commission)

"North and South have more interests in common on a medium and long-term basis than many have so far been able to recognize." (The Brandt Report, 1980)[21]

The general philosophy of development policy has been to integrate less developed countries into the international division of labour. This strategy will only work if international trade is increasing. The biggest help for developing countries would be a 3-4 per cent growth rate in Europe (without protectionism). Such an expansion would enhance real exports of developing countries, while increasing demand would lead to higher raw material prices. Relief of the debt burden and more development aid for the poorest countries is also urgently needed.

The Brundtland Report demonstrates the close link between environmental damage and the economic situation in developing countries. Poverty is the main cause of environmental problems. There appears to be a close connection between poverty and overexploitation of soil and forests, as well as water contamination. Environmental concerns become less urgent when day-to-day survival is at stake. Economic recession in the Third World thus contributes indirectly to extensive and irreversible environmental damage (such as deforestation in tropical regions) which affects us all.

Higher "qualitative" economic growth would help avert both the debt crisis and environmental disasters. The debt crisis threatens young democracies, much as youth unemployment poses risks for democracy in Europe.

Developing countries have great potential for rapid growth, and their high propensity to consume and invest gives them an important role in generating economic expansion worldwide.

Europe would fulfil the objective of meeting Third World needs, as well as improving her own economic situation, by increasing development aid to the poorest countries with low credit-worthiness, by increased lending to the debt-ridden countries, by efforts to help stabilize raw material prices and by measures to reduce interest rates.

Additional finance also needs to be used more efficiently than in the past. The failure of many development policies ("cathedrals in the desert") has been due to the lack of involvement and follow-up from lenders and donors. Investment projects need careful planning and must be preceded by training and monitored afterwards for much longer than previously considered necessary. All this means that development assistance demands a great deal of qualified manpower, both in donor and recipient countries. The supply of suitable manpower can be a more important bottleneck to efficient development assistance than the supply of funds.

The fifteen most indebted countries are not in the lowest income group and no feasible increase in official development aid will solve their problems. To tackle the debt issue there needs to be higher economic growth as well as lower long-run interest rates both for new finance and for restructuring existing debt.

Fears that more help for developing countries will simply intensify competition between Europe and the newly industrializing countries are misplaced. Europe's industrial future should not lie in competing with these countries by lowering wages, but rather in appropriate long-term policies for technology and innovation that permit higher real wages without eroding international competitiveness.

It is idealistic to assume that development aid is a purely humanitarian task which ought not to carry with it any economic advantages for the donor countries.Such a notion existed in the past, mainly in Scandinavian countries. However, it is increasingly apparent that development assistance can be much more efficient if its mutually beneficial economic aspects are acknowledged. Both donor and receiver countries can benefit, though in general the superior negotiating capacity and knowledge of donor countries' companies have given them the greatest advantage. A better balance could be achieved through firmer control by donor governments. Controls should certainly also ensure that funds do not end up in the pockets of ruling elites and that environmental protection is not neglected.

Environmental charges imposed on companies in industrialized countries have induced some to move factories to the Third World, or dump their toxic wastes in poor countries, giving rise to pollution problems which also may effect the environment in the rest of the world in the long run. International agreement to prevent "environmental dumping" is urgently needed.

Development assistance cannot, however, be confined to large-scale industrial and construction projects. Development assistance needs to be "twisted" towards establishing basic preconditions for development, such as education and training, health care, family planning and the provision of essential food (without discouraging indigenous food production).

One of the most efficient methods of development assistance would be to open Western markets fully to the exports of developing countries. The trend has been in the other direction: industrial countries have increased protection. Studies by the United Nations Conference on Trade and Development show that so-called preference tariffs for developing countries are sometimes higher than normal tariffs. Poor economies also face more extensive non-tariff restrictions of trade (import quotas and so on). According to UNCTAD, 26 per cent of imports from developing countries faced non-tariff barriers in 1986, compared to 21 per cent of imports from industrialized countries. Restrictions were most severe for clothing and textiles and of growing importance for steel.

The Commission would endorse proposals for a massive transfer of resources to developing countries, though this should be weighted more towards manpower resources and less towards capital resources than others have advocated. Development aid as practised so far permits neither a substantial nor a continuous development of the recipient countries' economic potential; the development of basic infrastructure is an absolute precondition for generating self-sustaining growth, which must be accompanied by measures enabling countries to make optimum use of available credit facilities or to obtain other forms of additional financing.

We would urge a new concept of development assistance resembling in some respects the Marshall Plan for Europe. There ought to be systematic, assured long-term co-operation between developing and industrialized countries. While there can be no objection to bilateral development assistance, it should not be the only form of aid.

Policy-makers and the public should take account of political and social aspects of North–South trade and debt relations. It must be in the interests of the North to see stability and orderly democratic processes succeed in the South. A solution of the debt crisis would undoubtedly strengthen the blossoming democracies in Latin America. Conversely, the military could find ample excuse to oust civilian government if the problems are not solved.

A recent opinion poll of over 11,500 people in the Community suggests support for more Third World aid is growing. Three-quarters thought EC aid should be encouraged, 7 percentage points more than in a similar survey three years earlier.[22]

Employment effects

"Developing countries offer vast employment opportunities for us. But before we can grasp them, we need a long-term strategy to solve the debt crisis." (Raymond Barre, at the Paris meeting of the Commission)

Like environmental protection, development assistance in the broadest sense of the word—that is, including the improvement of trade relations with the developing countries—has considerable employment potential. Investments directed at the economic and social infrastructure of these countries, financed through a highly flexible system of loans, would result in a substantial increase in demand. To guarantee that the new infrastructure functions as intended will often mean a very long commitment Much of the demand from developing countries will be for highly qualified manpower. A formula is needed to ensure that the provision of management assistance does not clash with the sovereignty of the recipient country.

Much has been made of job losses caused by exports of the South to the North, whereas little or no attention has been paid to the jobs created by exports from North to South. Any assessment of North–South trade relations must take account of the impact on employment in the North resulting from developing countries' fluctuating import capacity.

Following the pioneering work of the ILO in its World Employment Programme, UNIDO conducted a series of studies analyzing the employment effects in major industrialized countries of trade in manufactured products. The latest of these studies examines direct and indirect employment gains and losses due to exports and imports for the six leading industrial nations. It found that: "In net terms, trade with the South has resulted in increased employment in the North."[23] These gains were most pronounced in Japan, but were positive for all six countries. Net employment gains were concentrated in the fast-growing industries (mainly machinery, electrical machinery and chemicals). Most job losses occurred in a limited number of "mature" industries (mainly textiles and clothing, food, leather and wood products).

The earlier mentioned study carried out by the Nordic and German trade union confederations[24] concluded that if the affluent countries fulfilled the UN target by granting at least 0.7 per cent of their GDP in development aid for two years, this would create about 1.9 million jobs in the OECD area and millions of jobs in the Third World. Today only Norway, the Netherlands, Denmark, Sweden and France (if aid to its Overseas Departments and Territories is included) meet this target.

The effects of the debt crisis are of immediate concern for policy-makers grappling with unemployment. One, currently hypothetical but nevertheless possible, scenario concerns the potential employment effects of a "collapse" of the world financial system, that might follow the formation of an effective "debtors' cartel". Another—more immediate, but related—aspect is the need for developing countries to cut their import bills and boost exports simply to keep up with servicing their debts. Yet the surge of protectionism and tighter economic policies with high interest rates in the North has made it all the harder for debtor countries to achieve this objective. With many of them caught in a vicious circle, a mutually acceptable solution of the debt problem is all the more important, not least because of the unforeseeable consequences in the absence of such an agreement. The Baker plan to obtain new money for debtor countries has failed in many respects. What is needed is debt relief; an actual reduction in the absolute level of debt. Presently, much of the savings in Europe and Japan goes to consumption in the US. Everybody would be better off in the long run if it went to investments in the developing countries.

While the above issues require the urgent attention of policy-makers in North and South, another effect of the debt crisis is already upon us: the loss of employment in Europe and other OECD countries due to the dramatic decline in import capacities of developing countries.

The positive employment impact of improved trade relations with the Third World is unquestionable. The role of development assistance can be exemplified by a specific railway project: existing branch terminal lines are to be interlinked in the West African region. Since the branch terminal lines do not now link up, some countries cannot make use of rail transport to convey their products to the ports. Obviously, the additional investment will enormously enhance the efficiency of the railway network and bring important economic benefits to the region. Many such projects exist which would provide employment opportunities for both indigenous and European manpower.

Part V: Economic and Political Feasibility of a Programme for Europe

"We are depriving the young of their possibility to protest by saying that no one is responsible for unemployment." (David Lea, at the first Vienna meeting of the Commission)

1. Barriers to expansionary policies

Governments in the leading European countries have mostly been reluctant to take action to reduce unemployment. They argue that their task is to improve the functioning of markets. A reduction of unemployment will then come of itself, without the drawbacks that an active policy for creating employment is supposed to bring. So far however this expected reduction of unemployment has not materialized.

Traditionally, macroeconomic policies have been used to achieve full employment and microeconomic policies to fight inflation. The new orthodoxy maintains instead that monetary and fiscal tightening can cut inflation rates without influencing unemployment in the long run.

Unemployment is seen as a consequence of labour market inflexibility.

Supply-side and long-run considerations have certainly been too much neglected in the past, but in stressing these the new orthodoxy neglects the role of demand and macroeconomic planning. There are basically three ways to increase effective demand: deficit spending, stimulating private investment and income redistribution (to lower income groups with a higher propensity to consume). During the last decade, as a consequence of the monetarist revolution, all three have been used to restrain demand even after unemployment rose dramatically.

Discretionary fiscal measures were restrictive in most European countries to curb the rise in budget deficits brought about by recession and increasing interest payments. Private investment was impeded by extremely high interest rates, and income was redistributed towards the wealthy through high interest on their assets and welfare cuts for the poor.

The redistributional effects of tight policies are evident: high interest rates favour the creditor and hurt the debtor. Thus they favour the old at the expense of the new—since new firms, new households and young developing countries are typically high debtors.

The world has now been left with three enormous problems: massive developing country indebtedness and high government debt in many countries of the industrialized world; an inappropriate industrial structure in Europe (too much mass production and heavy industry); and a vast surplus of labour. Faith in automatic market forces to push economies towards full employment has been dented for the second time this century. The only way out of this dilemma is to put the economies of Europe and Japan into a higher gear. Japan is already on its way.

Political obstacles

Political action to reduce unemployment is impeded by a long-term development which has sometimes been called the transition from a "pyramid society" to a "diamond society". When the majority of people felt threatened by unemployment, they were more easily united to vote in solidarity for expansionary policies, even if this would entail some risks. Now, the majority of citizens have quite secure and well-paid jobs and considerable financial assets. It is much more difficult to invoke a sense of solidarity with the less well situated or recruit a majority for an expansionary programme.

In addition, the long period of growth in the postwar decades and the establishment of full employment led to far-reaching and fundamental changes and the problems of adjustment. The massive influx of migrant workers created new pressures and tensions. Young people became more self-confident and the strong demand for highly qualified labour paved the way for student unrest. Employers began to fear a slackening of discipline among their workers: dismissal was made more difficult and lost its sting as a disciplinary measure, as those concerned were enthusiastically welcomed by competitors. The expansion of the school system led to more equal opportunities for children from different backgrounds and, together with rising female employment and shrinking unemployment, to more equal household incomes. High wage increases demonstrated the increased negotiating strength of organized labour. A growing segment of the population acquired a "middle class" lifestyle.

It is not surprising that after this redistribution of incomes and power, after a period of high inflation and a consequent devaluation of the civic virtue of saving, calls for stability became ever more strident. Price stability and budget stability also often mean stability of the social structure and of the distribution of incomes and opportunities. Persistent inflation, beyond its initial push such as a sharp rise in commodity prices, is essentially an expression of the battle between those seeking changes in income distribution and those seeking to preserve the *status quo*.

Rapid social change is unavoidable in times of high economic growth and full employment. If it exceeds a certain limit, insecurity is often the consequence. The pendulum then swings in the other direction towards tradition and the known.

In our view, the long period of weak growth in Europe, with all its adverse effects on the labour market, has persisted largely because of the reactions of important groups of the population, and their political representatives, to the social changes associated with full employment. These reactions may take a decade or more of pause and consolidation to fade, at the same time as world industrial crisis and mass unemployment begin to spur counter-forces. An important task of our Commission is to mobilize these counter-forces against unemployment.

Four main constraints

Apart from political obstacles four main objections are commonly advanced against a demand management policy for economic expansion and job creation. We believe these factors are no longer, if they ever were, fundamental constraints on government action to cut unemployment.

The first objection is that growth is not desirable because it creates environmental problems and imposes intolerable social strains through the need for structural change. However, as we have argued earlier, economic stagnation means fewer resources to improve the environment and cushion the impact of economic and social change. One unavoidable development in Europe is the ageing of the population, which will put a heavy burden on working people in years to come. High unemployment means that this burden must be carried by fewer people.

The second objection relates to inflation. In the minds of most people, this is probably the basic constraint on growth policies. Stagflation has been the dominant experience of the economies of the industrialized countries since the first oil price shock. Many have come to believe that efforts to stimulate growth must end in higher inflation. We maintain that controlling inflation through high unemployment is not an acceptable way to run a country's economy.

In restricting growth to cut inflation, productive resources are destroyed, mainly human capacity but also productive capital and organization. This is especially serious in view of the demands that the care of environment, population ageing and other urgent needs put on Europe's economies. Unemployment cannot be significantly reduced through policies confined to the labour market such as increased flexibility and more scope for market forces. New job openings on a massive scale are indispensable and cannot be achieved without an increase in total output.

The third objection is fiscal constraint, the argument being that fiscal expansion would give rise to problems in the longer run through government indebtedness and a rising interest burden. This view seems to be founded on the experiences of the 1970s, when demand expansion through fiscal policy in many countries covered the income loss caused by higher oil prices and thus did not translate into increased investment. An expansionary demand management policy must be formulated in such a way that it results in extra investment and higher productivity, resulting in increased tax returns.

The fourth objection relates to the balance-of-payments constraint. We have argued that this constraint can be minimized by international co-ordination of economic policies. The bad experiences associated with expansion policies in 1978-79 were caused by the Islamic revolution in Iran and the second oil price shock, which were unrelated to those policies.

2. International constraints

> "The level of economic integration in Europe is much higher than the level of political co-ordination." (Michele Salvati, at the Mallorca meeting of the Commission)

One of the main explanations for the slowdown in economic growth during the last 15 years, and of the poor showing of Europe in particular, lies with lack of co-ordination in policy-making at the European and world level.

In the 1930s, unemployment could more easily be handled as a national problem. Today, with deregulated financial markets and high export/import ratios in trade, international co-ordination is necessary to make an expansionary programme successful. The problem is that the level of economic integration is much higher than the willingness of governments to co-operate. The industrial economies have become tightly interwoven, which has made them dependent on each other and, more especially, on the strongest economic powers and financial centres. This interdependence limits the scope for autonomous economic policy. Big countries, particularly those with large current account surpluses, have more room for manoeuvre. But these countries have become less prepared to co-operate with each other in order to tackle unemployment. Some improvement in the G-7-co-operation in the last few years must however be noted. But unemployment does not seem to have been on their agenda so far.

Other ingredients have been important. Following the first oil shock few countries successfully developed institutions and rules of the economic game which could cope with the inflationary pressures of spiralling commodity prices in a fully-employed economy. For most European countries restrictive monetary and fiscal policies were the only available weapon against inflation. And structural changes were also undermining the virtuous circle of the postwar "Golden Age", spanning the period between the end of reconstruction and the first oil shock. These were related to the exhaustion of the "easy" sources of productivity growth in mass-production techniques, and the symmetrical exhaustion—in the most advanced countries, at least—of a consumption pattern based on cars and consumer durables, and all that went with them.

Leaving aside this last and controversial ingredient, we

discuss here the problem of international (and particularly European) economic integration and policy co-ordination. Incomes policy and inflation will be touched on in the next section.

Unusually fast growth and deepening economic integration went hand in hand in the immediate postwar period. Starting from the very low level of openness of the late 1940s, a level which was much lower than before the First World War, today even the biggest European economies have external trade sectors roughly equivalent to one-quarter of their national income. Much of this trade—usually around 60 per cent—is within the European Community or within Europe. This integration has been both a consequence and a cause of growth. At the international level, it stemmed from the same process of growing specialization and productivity on the one side, and of enlargement of markets on the other, that Adam Smith stressed in the context of a national economy. It has been suggested that most of the advantages of integration and specialization may have already been reaped in Europe. This is refuted in the Padoa-Schioppa and Cecchini reports[25] and by others. The prospect of further benefits is one of the reasons for the ambitious step in economic integration—completion of a unified internal market by 1992—that the EC has decided to take. We have no doubt that there is a strong link between economic integration, specialization, productivity, and potential growth. The lesson of the inter-war period is still fresh enough to remind us of the consequences of autarky and de-specialization.

Growing economic integration means growing interdependence. Failure to recognize this interdependence (or, rather, unwillingness to take the political steps that would follow from such recognition) is at the root of the present unsatisfactory state of affairs. There is still a minority view which maintains that all that is needed is a pure market co-ordination: simple and constant rules of money creation, perfectly free product and capital markets, a "clean" floating of exchange rates. Most informed observers, however, now agree that a closer co-ordination of national economic policies, within a stricter framework of rules, would allow a much stronger and less unbalanced growth of trade, both at the world and at the European level.

Between the late 1960s and the launch of the single market strategy, the only significant step in economic policy co-ordination at the EC level has been the estab-lishment of the European Monetary System in the late 1970s. In general, national economic policies remain unco-ordinated, both at the macroeconomic and at the microeconomic level. Fortunately, in postwar Europe this lack of co-ordination has not degenerated into the open, beggar-thy-neighbour warfare of the inter-war years, but it has produced self-defeating unilateral strate-gies.

This is most evident at the macroeconomic level, where the case for policy co-ordination rests on two simple advantages. The first is additional information, since the success of a national policy depends on a correct apprai-sal of what others will do. Would France have followed such an expansionary policy in 1981 if she had antici-pated the tightly restrictive stance of her main trading partners? The second, following on from the first, is the avoidance of overkill. Policies which appear sensible when pursued by one country may produce very unsatis-factory results when pursued by all. Europe fell into this trap in the early 1980s when simultaneous disinflation by most countries produced excessive and unexpected unemployment.

Unco-ordinated national strategies may also be self-defeating at the microeconomic level. Since micro-policies are mostly designed to increase efficiency and competitiveness in selected sectors of a very integrated economy, their success in bringing about growth and employment in a slow-growing world depends crucially on whether they can boost efficiency *vis-à-vis* competing countries. But if every country does the same, with roughly the same intensity and the same effectiveness, the competitive position of each participant will be unchanged. Such policies may then result in adverse effects in terms of misallocation of resources or worsened economic and social conditions. As with macroeconomic strategies, a single country cannot opt out of the game: it is forced to play, lest its competitiveness worsens *vis-à-vis* its trading partners. Two important examples suffice to illustrate the problem.

The first relates to industrial policies. Each country wishes to develop high-growth, high-valued-added, high-technology industries. The case for an active national industrial policy looks persuasive and politicians are easily seduced by it. But as a consequence, almost every country defends its own strategic industries—often identical—with all the means available. This can hamper a process of international integration and specialization which would collectively be very fruitful, in view of the continental scale which is often desirable to maximize the efficiency of these industries.

The second example concerns labour policies where, in order to gain somewhat doubtful employment advantages, countries are pursuing strategies that put in jeopardy Europe's traditions of decent industrial relations. It certainly can be argued that, in the early 1970s and in some countries in particular, industrial relations and wages became "too rigid". But the present enthusiasm for "flexibility" seen, with few exceptions, in labour legislation and collective bargaining all over Europe risks significantly worsening labour conditions, without providing any competitive advantage.

The disadvantages of non-coordination, the self-defeating nature of many national strategies, both macro and micro, are clear enough. Further steps in economic integration, if they are not accompanied by measures to improve economic policy co-ordination, are likely both to be relatively ineffective and to meet a justified political resistance at the national level. This is the important message of the Padoa-Schioppa Report, with which we fully agree.

A further liberalization in the goods and services markets would stimulate a further increase in specialization and productivity. It could thus provide a potential source of fresh growth, as has been pointed out in the Cecchini Report. Whether such growth will materialize, however, will depend on the existence of increasing aggregate demand, which in turn will depend on co-ordinated reflationary policies. Growth, moreover, will probably be unbalanced since the advantages of specialization are likely initially to benefit some regions more than others, and not necessarily those regions which most need to expand. (Within the European Community per capita income in the richest region, the Dutch province of Groeningen, is nearly six times that in the poorest, Trace in Greece.)

This conclusion applies still more strongly to liberalization of capital markets. In this case, the advantages of liberalization and specialization are more debatable than for the goods and services markets and will depend heavily on harmonization of national fiscal structures and strict co-ordination of monetary and fiscal policies. Otherwise capital will move not in search of the returns justified by specialization and efficiency, but in response to short-run, purely speculative, gains or differences in taxation, redistributional ambitions of governments and political security for capital.

Policy co-ordination is both a precondition for the political feasibility of a liberalization strategy and necessary ingredient for its benefits to be maximized.

The expansionary policy we are proposing will make any programme of further liberalization of product and capital markets more effective and more feasible. But if such a policy is pursued on a proper scale for a long period it may result in a trade deficit for Europe as a whole, and an unequal distribution of this deficit among European countries. Thus in order for a reflationary policy to be sustained, agreement must be reached on at least the three following issues.

(a) Europe *vis-à-vis* other continental areas. The overall European trade deficit will depend on the size of the expansionary push in Europe and on how other countries behave. If they opt for restriction, the European deficit could widen to an unsustainable level (though it would be counterbalanced by exchange rate changes). However, Europe now starts with a substantial surplus on current account (one per cent of GDP) and there is a long way to go before it runs into deficit. In addition, if Europe improves its competitive position through appropriate technological and educational policies in the medium term it can partly offset the tendency to trade deficits.

(b) The distribution of deficits and surpluses. Europe is a collection of states with very different levels of competitiveness and growth opportunities. The distribution of trade deficits and surpluses among European countries will depend on those structural factors and, crucially, on how the expansionary push itself is distributed. If it is confined to countries which most need to grow—but are also in weaker structural condition, with unsatisfactory current account and public sector balances—a European expansion would rapidly become unsustainable. Richer and stronger countries must also participate, perhaps even expanding first and faster. Overall expansion would then go hand in hand with a less unequal distribution of current account and public sector balances. This is another reason why we emphasize ecological and infrastructural investment as a key element of expansionary expenditure. Investment of this kind is socially and politically appealing in the richest European countries, and should help to create a consensus in support of an expansionary programme.

(c) Even if rich countries expand first and by more, intercountry imbalances will remain. A political agreement must be reached, therefore, on how to tackle such imbalances. Richer countries should be sympathetic to the need for faster growth in poorer countries or regions. If full monetary unification is impossible, some kind of pan-European bank should be created, with operating autonomy and funds commensurate with the scale of the task. We realize that the design of such an institution, its operating rules, its capitalization and its provision, would probably be the subject of considerable political conflict.

Conflict would stem firstly from divergent views about desirable social and economic outcomes. Different socioeconomic conditions and historical experience mean that countries—and regions and political groups within a country—may and do have divergent opinions about social and economic priorities. For some, the fight against unemployment has a lower priority than price stability. Ecological concerns are related less to the true gravity of the problems than to per capita incomes and national preoccupations. GDP growth is still the main goal of some politicians in some countries, but not of other countries or political groups. These differences —which could be greatly enlarged upon—pose many obstacles to the reduction of authority and autonomy in national policy-making. This is the second main source of conflict in attempting explicit co-ordination of economic policies. Politicians, especially in the smaller European countries, may be well aware that full autonomy and sovereign authority in monetary and fiscal matters is more apparent than real and that, when exercised, can cause the breakdown of co-ordination. In general, however, politicians are used to fighting for their priorities on familiar domestic turf and can be sceptical about the advantages of advancing their ideals and interests at an international level.

Full integration of capital markets within the European Community has now been agreed, as part of the drive for completion of the internal market. This will effectively mean the end of national independence in monetary policy-making. The result is however likely to be, not so much an open and co-operative discussion of what European monetary policy should be than a tacit agreement to let that policy be set by the strongest member states, notably West Germany.

This seems to us highly undesirable. Politicians must take the European arena much more seriously than they do now, and institutions must be strengthened or created that provide for democratic decision-making at that level.

We have stated that unemployment is the key European problem, and that its present level is morally and politically unacceptable. We have argued that technically feasible, socially useful, politically appealing programmes of investment are available that would strongly reduce the number of unemployed in Europe. We shall argue later that an expansionary policy can succeed in the context of our welfare state and industrial relations traditions, without creating unacceptable inflationary tensions. Here we acknowledge that an expansionary programme will encounter difficulties stemming from the disparity between the deep economic integration and weak political integration that characterizes European countries. But we also argue that economic difficulties can be overcome through stronger policy co-ordination. While this will shift the obstacles from the economic to the political level it is at this second level that the progressive political and social forces of Europe can contribute to more rational and humane policies.

3. The inflation constraint

"The only reason we have unemployment is that governments are using it to contain, or to reduce, inflation. Generally, governments will not admit this. But if you ever suggest doing anything to expand the economy, their answer will always be 'that's inflationary'."(Richard Layard, *How to Beat Unemployment*).[26]

The inflation-constraint argument rests on the assumption that there is a trade-off between inflation and unemployment in economic policy. However, much of the inflation of the 1970s was initiated by rising commodity prices—for agricultural commodities immediately before the first oil price shock, then by oil prices and many other commodities. They prompted increased wage claims to preserve living standards. In the 1980s falling commodity prices helped to reduce inflation rates. Some investigations suggest that as much as 70 per cent of inflation may have been caused by rising commodity prices. But undeniably there is also an important trade-off between inflation and unemployment. The wage explosion in Europe at the end of the 1960s that came before the surge in commodity prices also gave rise to higher inflation. In the US the relationship between wage increases and unemployment has been re-established at 1960s levels in recent years. But in Europe the trade-off remains considerably more unfavourable.

Nevertheless, at present, in most European countries, the utilization of equipment and labour is so low that there is considerable scope to reduce unemployment before inflation might again be dangerously stoked. The conditions for an expansionary programme could not be better than they are now: inflation rates are mostly very low, oil and other raw materials are in ample supply, and the low dollar is holding import prices down further.

But it is as important simultaneously to take measures to bring down the level of unemployment at which inflation becomes unacceptable. There are at least three ways in which the trade-off between inflation and unemployment can be improved: a stabilization of commodity prices (through buffer stocks and so on), labour market policies to prevent bottlenecks and equip the workforce for structural change, and an adequate incomes policy. In some of the Nordic countries and in Austria an explicit incomes policy has contributed considerably to overcoming stagflation. In West Germany, a tacit incomes policy has held wage claims down. Lower nominal wage demands may also permit higher increases in real wages, since they pave the way for stronger growth and faster improvements in productivity. We are, of course, conscious of the political and technical difficulties of all the three ways.

4. Financial aspects

"As much private finance as possible, as much public finance as necessary." (Edgar Plan, at the London meeting of the Commission)

"Today people do not accept high public debt." (Hans-Jurgen Krupp, at the London meeting of the Commission)

How to finance the proposed investment programme is a

complex question. It will vary from project to project and from country to country, according to political priorities and availability of funds.

The following ways need to be explored:

(a) *Financing through the private capital market.* Many large infrastructure projects may be financed by the capital market, though they need a large organizational effort.

The tunnel under the Channel is a good example of how private financing of infrastructure can work. It is noteworthy that government regulations prohibit a project in competition to the "Chunnel" for the next two decades. This example shows that more collaboration between the private and public sectors on infrastructure projects is possible and can provide an important additional source of investment finance. Investors will often insist on a free hand in fixing user fees, and sometimes guarantees by the State will be needed, particularly for very risky long-run projects.

(b) *Government financing.* Many projects can and should be financed by private capital. However, there is a wide range of projects that are not profitable on a private basis and must be financed by governments. Pollution control, for example, can only be financed by higher taxes on leaded petrol and other forms of energy, or by "compulsory levies", partly in the form of higher prices for the products of modified production processes. We favour an energy tax to finance investment in environmental protection. Such a tax would also provide an incentive for energy conservation and thereby reduce the demand for new power stations which are detrimental to the environment.

In general, government budgets must be restructured towards new priorities, such as environmental and technology policy. Apart from that the costs of new projects must always be compared with the total fiscal savings from a reduction in unemployment, bearing in mind that more dynamic growth will generate extra tax revenue and social security contributions.

(c) *Supranational investment financing.* Innovative ideas in the financial area are urgently needed to fund investment projects by both the public and the private sector which are currently blocked. One idea, the setting up of a supranational bank, is developed below.

As important national investment projects have been completed, the need and desirability of continuing with more public mega-projects are being increasingly questioned. On the supranational level, however, many valuable projects remain unrealized. The European road system is a patchwork arising from different national views on how cities and regions should be linked. Public procurement, for example of telecommunications equipment, is often linked to national industrial interests, while harmonization of national systems is treated as a secondary problem. Even the activities of the European Investment Bank (EIB), a supranational institution within the framework of the European Community, have primarily a national dimension, since they finance projects designed and developed mainly by national administrations.

The lack of an authority to secure the financing of supranational investment may be one reason why multi-country projects are given low priority. However, the appearance of the "Chunnel", the combined bridge-tunnel project to connect Sweden and Denmark, and the network of high-speed railway connections between the main European cities (TGV) demonstrate a growing interest in multi-country projects. The establishment of a completely free internal market within the European Community is likely to direct priorities further towards such projects.

Multi-country projects require multi-country financing. Thus it may be worthwhile to explore the setting up of a supranational intergovernmental institution, say the "Bank for Infrastructure" (BFI). The BFI could either be a new independent bank—probably better—or it could operate as a branch of an existing institution, such as the European Investment Bank. It should be noted that the EIB has already committed 1 billion ECU in 1987 for the Eurotunnel "Chunnel" project, because it was considered to be of exceptional importance for the European transport network.

There is no necessity for monetary financing by governments or central banks of the activities of the BFI. Efficient co-operation between the private and the public sector could raise substantial funds. Interested governments as well as private groups might participate in providing its capital. The Bank's executive board would select projects and examine their profitability. If the need presented itself, the Bank's borrowing activities could be expanded.

To avoid excessive recourse to certain domestic capital markets, the BFI should utilize to the fullest extent the possibilities of the Eurobond market, where as much as US$140.5 billion of new issues were raised in 1987. Borrowing in ECU is advocated beside borrowing in US dollars, in Yen or in any particular currency, so that exchange risks can be reduced.

One major problem would have to be solved —how the BFI would raise revenues to guarantee repayment of principal and payment of interest, so that investments in BFI bonds were deemed profitable by financial markets. One possibility is that the group undertaking the project would pay off its loans to the BFI from the revenues earned from user fees. Of course, the BFI would have an advantage over private investment groups in raising funds on the international bond markets as it would, to some extent at least, benefit from the support of governments and their guarantees. In some cases, the imposition of user fees may not be desirable. But if the projects are profitable, a positive effect on economic growth and fiscal revenues can be expected. In that event, the participating countries might agree on the transfer of some of the extra revenues to the BFI.

Developments in the capital markets over the past decade or so show that financing and funding need not constitute a bottleneck. An appropriate mix of public direction and guidance with private initiative and entrepreneurship can go a long way towards achieving the goal of promoting employment through a substantial expansion of infrastructure investment.

Growth is necessarily connected with an increase in money and credit. However, the international capital market is awash with liquidity. Thus, there would be no need to create additional liquidity generally in Europe, at least not in the initial stage of an employment creation programme and probably not for many years to come, provided that private capital wants to stay in Europe and does not run to the US. But a redistribution of credit to countries, particularly in southern Europe, which have been forced to adopt restrictive policies because of external and internal imbalances, will be an important part of the programme.

International capital markets and expansionary policies

> "A major obstacle to full employment policy is freedom of speculative capital movements." (David Lea, at the second Vienna meeting of the Commission)

There is a fundamental conflict between the financial markets that have traditionally placed more emphasis on a strong currency and a low rate of inflation, and the industrial sector which has emphasized growth and employment. Winston Churchill, then Chancellor of the Exchequer, observed in 1925 that:

> "The Governor (of the Bank of England) shows himself perfectly happy in the spectacle of Britain possessing the finest

credit in the world simultaneously with a million and a quarter unemployed. . . . I would rather see Finance less proud and Industry more content.''

International capital tends to vote with its feet. And while there has always been this external constraint on domestic demand management, the situation has changed dramatically since the official dismantling of the Bretton Woods system of fixed exchange rate parities in 1973. The phenomenal growth of a large Eurodollar/ Eurocurrency market followed by deregulation of financial markets in many countries has made possible vast and rapid movements of funds. Over 90 per cent of the volume of day-to-day transactions in the foreign exchange markets is now accounted for by speculative capital transfers, on recent guesstimates. Less than ten per cent represents international trade transactions. Thus the focus of interest has shifted from the trading (or current) account to the capital account of the balance of payments. When a government tries to follow traditional Keynesian remedies to fight unemployment at home by increasing expenditure, it may immediately endanger the balance of payments position, not so much because of spillover of demand into a trade deficit on current account, but because of large financial outflows (often in the expectation of a weakening currency) on capital account.

This in turn can have a paralyzing effect on demand management. National autonomy in pursuing economic policies for fighting unemployment is being eroded by the increasing degree of freedom enjoyed by the international private financial sector. This serves to emphasize the need for co-ordinated efforts on a European scale to fight unemployment rather than leaving it to individual nations.

Part VI: Labour Market Strategies

Even if higher growth rates are achieved it will be difficult and take a long time to reduce long-term unemployment substantially in decaying industrial areas. An active manpower policy will always be needed to smooth structural changes and to squeeze the most out of efforts to increase employment with the minimum of negative side-effects.

The employment content of growth has markedly increased during the last decade, due to weak investment, low productivity growth and the structural shift to the service sector. Ways of further increasing the employment content of growth are fairly limited, if the reduction of working time is left aside. The American route of "working poor" (very low minimum wages and low unemployment benefits) has been rejected by the Commission. A retardation of technical progress to raise employment is also undesirable for reasons of international competitiveness.

An expansion of public employment (as in the 1970s) has to face the psychological limits of taxation. There may be some room for manoeuvre in semi-public areas like health services, environment protection and culture. Generally, however, higher public investment in infrastructure with positive side-effects on the private propensity to invest is preferable to higher public consumption and employment.

1. The role of manpower policies

"Labour market policy has been the main instrument to fight unemployment in the Nordic countries." (Georg Fischer, at the second Vienna meeting of the Commission)

The model of an active labour market policy is Sweden, which has a much higher percentage of the labour force in labour market programmes than other European countries—between $2\frac{1}{2}$ and 4 per cent. Of particular interest are the training programmes for the unemployed. Nearly all unemployed people in Sweden—with the exception of older people—undergo training to prevent discouragement and demoralization, and jobs have been secured for nearly all of them. Two-thirds have found jobs for which the training was relevant, the rest have turned to other occupations, sometimes after more than one training course. Thus very few are becoming long-term unemployed in Sweden, only around 5 per cent of total unemployment. Training is geared mainly to retraining for other, more qualified jobs than those previously held. This was of importance for the restructuring of the Swedish economy.

Finland has introduced a work or retraining guarantee in some provinces for those unemployed for more than a year. The young unemployed are given this guarantee after a few months of fruitless job-search.

No one contests the need for improved education and training. But improvements are often very slow to

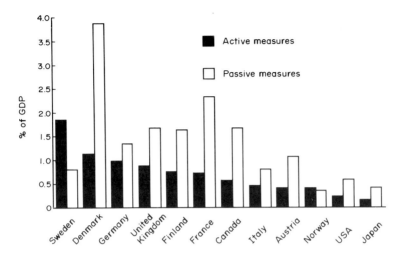

Source: OECD, *Employment Outlook*

FIGURE 4. Importance of labour market policy in different countries

implement. Figure 4 shows expenditures for passive
(income maintenance) and active labour market policies
in different countries in relation to the rate of unemployment the same year. In countries with high youth unemployment those with incomplete formal education and
training are the main victims. Their educational failures
often date back to primary school. Thus reform of
vocational training would not be enough. This is
especially the case in countries with theory-overburdened
and elitist school systems. It is also an important but
often neglected task to see that education and training are
adapted to present and future needs and not to historical
ones.

Improved education and increased flexibility can help
fill vacancies. To some extent, the amount of vacancies
also depends on the supply of suitably skilled labour. If

no trained workers are available, employers may refrain from making investments that require trained workers.

Labour market policy—influencing the functioning and organization of the labour market—needs to play a supportive role in the realization of any expansion programme. In this sense, labour market policy should be designed to help overcome possible obstacles to such a programme. Through training for the "unemployable" and reduction of bottlenecks, labour market policy can promote employment and hence growth. In contrast to the short-run relief provided by early retirement schemes labour market policy is a long-run device to improve economic development.

In recent years, the development of labour resources has been greatly obstructed by high unemployment. Unemployment as such is of course a waste of human potential. The unemployed, particularly those out of work for a long time, and young people without stable employment, do not have the opportunity to develop their abilities, and may find what skills and abilities they have subject to a process of degradation and demotivation. At the same time, companies have cut back on their own training efforts, sometimes for cost reasons, sometimes because of the feeling that with such high levels of joblessness suitable skilled labour ought to be available on the market.

This could lead to bottlenecks in the labour market if labour demand starts to increase more strongly. Moreover, studies show that many of the most promising production possibilities—whether in industry or the service sector—have a high demand for qualified, flexible, service-oriented and innovative skilled labour. There is no automatic mechanism that will respond with an appropriate supply of labour. In particular in the areas of environmental protection and new information services, there appears to be a lack of suitable training and development capacity.

The wide regional disparities in unemployment in Europe must also be taken into account. In West Germany, for instance, unemployment rates in the north are up to three or four times as high as in the prospering south. The situation in Great Britain is very similar. To avoid regional bottlenecks in the wake of economic expansion, labour market policy needs to improve the qualifications and mobility of workers.

Another consideration relates to changes in the sex composition of the labour force. The increase in women's participation rates is likely to continue. This growing female workforce is far better trained than in the past. But the full range of job and career possibilities is not open to many women. If possible bottlenecks—for example, shortages of qualified skilled workers—are to be overcome, a labour market policy must aim to lower the barriers between male and female employment.

Labour market policies are essential to remedy the effects of a long period of high unemployment, which has left certain groups on the margins of the labour market, due either to changes in the demand for labour or personal handicaps: the long-term unemployed, those with repeated spells of unemployment, physically or socially handicapped persons, young people who have not been able to integrate themselves into the employment system, single mothers, women without occupational or professional training, members of minorities, children of immigrants. Many have become discouraged and have stopped actively looking for work. Without any claim to state financial support they have lost contact with the employment system and its institutions. These groups, which already account for a large share of unemployment, are socially stigmatized; by implication they are considered to be unemployed not as a consequence of low growth rates, but rather because of their own failure. There is thus little readiness to hire them even under more favourable conditions.

Labour market policy must therefore have a corrective function, assisting particularly vulnerable groups to gain access to the labour market and benefit from employment opportunities in ordinary workplaces or specifically arranged relief works and sheltered workshops. In Sweden, the employment of the handicapped, either through sheltered workshops under public sponsorship or through wage subsidies to private firms or municipalities is one of the most important elements of labour market policy, affecting alone over 1.5 per cent of the labour force.

Labour market policy should emphasize the following strategies:

(a) *Provision of efficient and comprehensive labour information and employment services, on which the implementation of policy depends.* There needs to be an extensive network of local employment offices. In some countries, labour exchanges are now computerized so that every office has access to every job opening nationwide or at least regionwide.

(b) *Promotion of training by companies to satisfy the higher levels of skill demanded by future production and to create an innovative workforce that will enable the company to maintain or increase market share.* Measures should include advice to companies on implementing corporate training, and support for an initiation of co-operation between companies (such as joint training and development centres). This aspect is especially important for small and medium-sized companies, since their limited funds and planning capacity make it difficult for them to provide adequate training facilities. In addition, training policy should ensure that all employees have access to educational and training programmes, and that enterprises do not, for example, discriminate directly or indirectly against women or unskilled workers. The improvement of skills through training creates an asset for the economy as a whole, while the individual employer can lose his workers to competitors. Thus a good deal of the costs of training and retraining should be provided by society. In some countries, like France, there is a training tax that is reimbursed to those firms which satisfy training requirements.

(c) *Promotion of general further education.* Trends in modern society demand a citizenry capable of adapting to technological and social changes affecting not only their jobs but all aspects of their lives. This in turn requires a well-functioning system of further education, both vocational and general. Policy measures should include: creation of adequate institutions for further education and full utilization of existing training facilities; financial help where needed for people undergoing further education; and concentration on groups which have traditionally been denied access to further education, including those with no previous professional or vocational training, people with family care commitments and members of minorities.

(d) *Concentration of demand-oriented measures of labour market policy on high-unemployment areas and on disadvantaged groups, notably the long-term unemployed and young jobless people.* Such measures should comprise integration and training benefits as well as direct job creation measures. Labour market policy should also tear down barriers which could otherwise inhibit employment growth. Demand-oriented labour market measures should be geared to stimulating permanent employment of those who would otherwise find themselves bypassed by increased job opportunities. Suitable measures should apply equally to the private and public sectors.

To conclude: The social goal of labour market policy is mainly to improve the position of the most vulnerable and help them to secure jobs corresponding to their acquired qualifications and abilities. In economic terms, labour market policy can increase total employment through better training and higher mobility and thereby reducing wage and price pressure. And it has a crucial microeconomic role in geting the right men and women to the right jobs. Labour market measures should thus generally be available for everyone who wants to change jobs. In this context, efficient employment services have a key role to play.

2. Reduction of working time

"The combination of shorter working hours and higher flexibility is a good way to bridge employers' and employees' interests." (Karl-Heinz Brodersen, at the second Vienna meeting of the Commission)

A reduction of working time as an instrument of employment policy was a controversial issue in the Commission's discussions.

The subject of shorter working hours has gained current prominence because five years of moderate economic growth in Europe have failed to cut unemployment. Further, in the last decade reductions in working hours have been much smaller than previously. Some members of the Commission have accordingly argued that this retardation has added to unemployment, and that little dent can be made in the level of joblessness unless working hours are cut. They also argued that working time had been reduced steadily during this century and the trend ought to continue. Reduction of working time should also be an important long-run goal contributing to a higher quality of life.

More rapid economic growth would provide scope for shorter hours that could increase the number of jobs created. A reduction of working time could thus be regarded as a means of "twisting" growth by making it more employment-intensive.

Other members of the Commission stressed that a reduction in working time is not a solution to economic problems (of certain regions and industries) because it can do no more than redistribute, probably to only a small extent, the limited number of jobs available.

Small reductions of working time (say, of one hour a

week) would not have a large effect on employment because they can easily be offset by higher productivity, as the experience of France and other countries seems to suggest. Big reductions of working time (for example, from 40 to 35 hours) would produce substantial employment effects, but would oblige existing employees to make large sacrifices. A five-hour reduction in weekly hours would lead to a marked cut in workers' real wages, brought about by wage restraint or higher prices. This cut in real wages is virtually inevitable since real national income would at best remain unchanged. Such a "sacrifice for solidarity" may have some appeal at times of high unemployment, but there is a danger that cutting working hours could actually hinder subsequent economic expansion. This could happen through pushing up unit labour costs and thus hurting competitiveness—especially if the hours cut is not implemented on a European level—or through contributing to shortages of qualified manpower.

However, shorter working hours will not automatically increase labour costs for the enterprise, even if workers receive the same pay as before. In practice, extra costs may be offset by reduced claims for fringe benefits, better working conditions or wages in coming years, or by an increase of productivity (though this will dampen the employment effect).

Past experience seems to suggest that a reduction of working time can help to increase employment if international competitiveness is taken into consideration. However, it does not help very much in reducing unemployment in declining regions.

Faced with the lack of success of other policies reducing unemployment, trade unions in Europe continue to call for cuts in working time, while employers want greater flexibility in hours and work organization. Both are compatible, even complementary.

More flexible working hours

> "Electronic equipment, in particular, requires high utilization rates, since it becomes obsolete within a few years—not because it is old, but because it is superseded by more efficient equipment." (Ferdinando Borletti, at the Paris meeting of the Commission)

Greater flexibility in hours (such as continuous shift-working) can raise the rate of capacity utilization and hence productivity, with expensive equipment used in a more efficient way. This would reduce cost pressures resulting from shorter working hours. More flexible working hours could also reduce bottlenecks for skilled workers. However, the would also reduce the short-run employment effects.

Greater flexibility in working arrangements would invalidate the criticism that shorter working hours would reduce the quality of life since public and private services would operate for less time (for instance, a five-day week in shops). Availability of public services should certainly not be reduced any more. It does not make sense to pay billions for libraries and museums and open them only for the non-working population.

More flexible working arrangements comprise part-time work, annual working hours, flexible opening hours, a right to paid educational leave, and so on. There is a considerable scope for more flexibility. In the EC 13.5 per cent of the employed work part-time and only 10-20 per cent of them would like to work longer hours.

More flexibility in working hours is not only desired by employers, but also by many workers (especially younger ones).

Early retirement has been in the past a way to cut unemployment but in the future the ageing of the population means that the working capacity of older people will be needed to guarantee a decent standard of living for the increasing number of retired. Early retirement should now be made easier only for special groups: those doing heavy manual work, the sick, and so on. In any event, longer life expectancy would suggest a longer rather than a shorter working life. A more flexible transition to retirement could be an important element of flexible working time, which could take account of the economic situation and individual factors. It is hard to understand why labourers who begin their heavy, health-damaging work at the age of 16 should have the same retirement age as university graduates. In some professions, many workers of 60 cannot perform their job adequately; in others people have much to offer by way of skills and experience, which society cannot afford to dispense with.

3. Labour market flexibility and security

"Does not history show that social progress is the friend, not the enemy, of economic progress?" (Peter Coldrick, at the third Vienna meeting of the Commission)

No one is contesting the need for flexibility in a changing world, only the means of obtaining it. We certainly contest the idea that greater flexibility must be achieved by way of more inequality and insecurity. The brain-power labour market is much more heterogeneous than that of muscle-power, which greatly increases the transaction costs of flexibility (the costs of job moves and so on). Furthermore, increased inequalities in incomes and working conditions, for instance as part of incentive programmes, can result in more conflict in the workplace and this may be much more detrimental in brain-power than in muscle-power dominated production. Much of Japan's economic superiority seems to stem from a more successful transition from muscle-power to brain-power production.

It is important to note that the recent comprehensive review of the European labour market by the Brookings Institution, *Barriers to European Growth*,[27] concludes that there is "only limited evidence for barriers to growth on the supply side of the labour market".

There is a trade-off between flexibility and security. In essence, the postwar European economy developed on the basis of a broad social consensus, which institutionalized five "labour rights" in the context of an essentially "consensus" model involving active state regulation of social and economic affairs. These labour rights were:

(a) labour market security—a state commitment to full employment;

(b) income security—earnings protected by minimum wage machinery, unions playing an important role in the formulation of policy, insurance-based social security, and taxes to reduce (or check the growth of) income inequality;

(c) employment security—with regulations on hiring and firing, pre-notification of redundancy, the imposition of penalties on employers for "unfair dismissal", and so on;

(d) work security—through health and safety regulations, limits on working time, unsociable hours, and so on; and

(e) job security—through the tolerance of demarcation practices and barriers to skill dilution, craft boundaries and job qualifications, though this differs substantially between countries.

This last right was less accepted than the other four, but was nevertheless entrenched in "middle-class" professions such as the law and architecture, and among technically skilled workers. These various rights also represented costs to enterprises. Their acceptable continuation depended mainly on fairly stable economic growth.

Since the early 1970s, the whole employment scene has been radically transformed. This transformation process has been accompanied by the ideological restoration of monetarism and supply-side economics, which despite severe setbacks in their practical applications remain influential in some of the more important European governments.

According to the supply-side economists, it is because European labour markets are rigid and "sclerotic" that mass unemployment has arisen and persisted. Supply-side economics may highlight important long-run factors that have often been neglected in the past. But it does not provide a satisfactory explanation of what has happened to unemployment. Supply-siders argue that the remedies lie in decentralizing wage bargaining and weakening union power, dismantling minimum wage machinery, removing employment protection, widening wage differentials, cutting non-wage labour costs and income taxes. However, labour market flexibility has grown enormously in many parts of Europe in the past decade. So has unemployment. It is therefore hard to blame labour market rigidities for rising unemployment.

The evidence casts considerable doubt on the assertions of the supply-siders. For example, employment protection regulations do not seem to have been a major deterrent to employment as such. Structural development has not been more favourable in countries with little employment protection (e.g. Denmark). Regulations may, however, have altered the pattern of employment, encouraging the use of temporary labour, part-timers and subcontracting rather than regular, full-time workers. In addition, the alleged decline in labour mobility in Europe is partly illusory and partly a reflection of high unemployment rather than a cause of it.

Nominal and real wage flexibility are not positively correlated with decentralized, market-oriented wage determination systems. The efficacy of greater relative wage flexibility (essentially, higher wage differentials) in creating jobs is doubtful. Lower wages in the steel and textile industries, for example, would not solve their long-term problems, but would postpone necessary structural adjustments and push unemployment onto other (less developed) countries. In Sweden, a very good employment record has been associated with small and decreasing wage differentials and an efficient labour market policy.

As for the claim that a lack of training has been a major cause of "structural" unemployment, it is just a claim. Everybody can agree that genuine training for technical and professional competence is wholly desirable. But as a "key solution" to unemployment, one should be sceptical. That said, unlike subsidies to preserve employment in declining industries, retraining policies are a way to promote structural change, and make it easier to fill the vacancies that exist. In the long run, investment in human capital can be regarded as job creating in the same way as physical investment.

Implementation of the above-mentioned security rights may sometimes have led to unnecessary rigidities. The objective should be to provide labour market security rather than job security—that is, the right to work but not necessarily always in the same job. Not unnaturally, in conditions of mass unemployment, trade unions and workers have tended to conflate the two. This in turn has reinforced the backlash, so that the present tendency is towards more flexibility in all areas, useful or not.

The view that union restrictive practices and atavistic behaviour have contributed to rising unemployment is often dressed up in a respectable economic language. Some unions may have been very defensive in the wake of rising unemployment, but so-called union power has been on the wane in many parts of Europe for a long time. In any case, those countries in which unionization has been highest have maintained higher levels of employment.

Greater labour market flexibility may increase the chances of filling job vacancies but it will scarcely increase the number of vacancies available. We would argue that Europe does not need to reduce real wages to compete with newly industrialized countries. What is required are technical and organizational innovations to maintain and increase high income levels. The dismantling of bureaucratic and anti-competitive regulations would help in this respect.

The American experience

"The question of wages is not the central problem for industrialists, flexibility seems to be more important." (Karl-Heinz Brodersen, German industrialist, at the second Vienna meeting of the Commission)

The employment record of the United States is often used to disparage the performance of European labour markets and unemployment. A few points are worth noting.

Productivity growth has lagged in the United States, including in manufacturing. Thus, while a given increment in economic growth has resulted in much more employment growth in the US than in Europe, long-term competitiveness has declined. The costs of lower competitiveness have been partly borne by wages, which have fallen in real terms.

Many people argue that the European labour market should become like the American one—with more flexible wages (downward) and with more mobile workers. However, some recent studies cast doubt on the assumption that labour mobility in Europe is low and suggest that an increase in mobility would not help much in a situation where unemployment is widespread over regions and qualifications.

The notion that high mobility and flexibility in the United States underpin lower unemployment fails to explain why US unemployment during the 1950s and 1960s was much higher than in Europe. At that time, American labour market economists came to Europe to study the advantages of European labour market systems. Now the position is reversed.

The drawbacks of the American labour market are highlighted in a recent Harvard study,[28] which paints a sombre picture of social developments in recent years: 32 million Americans ($13\frac{1}{2}$ per cent) have incomes below the official poverty level, and their numbers have increased by 8 million since 1978.

Even as the economy has been growing, increasing numbers of Americans have been pushed onto the breadline. The distribution of the benefits of growth has been highly uneven, with little impact on the nation's 20 million hungry citizens. Income disparities in the United States are the widest for 40 years.

The theory espoused by the US administration, that tax cuts for the rich would "trickle down" to the population as a whole, has not been borne out in practice. Most severely hit by poverty are blacks, Hispanics and women. Half of all poor households in the US are headed by women.

Many of the people living in poverty are "working poor", whose incomes from full-time jobs remain below the poverty line. There are now nearly 7 million "working poor", 50 per cent more than in 1978. Many workers displaced from the mining, steel and oil industries entered the treadmill of low-wage jobs ("hamburger wages") and/or long-term unemployment. Federal minimum wages were last increased under President Carter, since when consumer prices have risen by 32 per cent. The results of the Harvard study raise serious doubts as to the suitability for Europe of the American model of high wage and labour market flexibility.

The "working poor" in the United States are the

equivalent to the unemployed in Europe. A participant of one of our meetings argued that he would rather be unemployed in Germany than "working poor" in the United States.

The Japanese experience

A number of influential voices have argued that if only European labour markets and employment practices were like those in Japan, we would be on our way to solving the European unemployment crisis. In addition, Japanese multinationals are rapidly expanding their presence in Europe, exporting with them their organizational structures and personnel practices. A couple of points are worth making.

Some economists and international organizations have claimed that the "flexible" Japanese payment system —low base wages and profit-related bonuses—has preserved employment stability and full employment. Most influential in that vein recently has been Martin Weitzman.[29] Various European governments are actively promoting "profit-related pay". Yet the evidence does not support the Weitzman thesis that the bonus pay system in Japan has been a major contributor to high and stable employment.

Japan has a "two-tier" labour force, with only about two-fifths in quasi-lifetime employment covered by such base-plus-bonus wage payments. Moreover, employment stability in Japan has been less than perceived. Much of the real unemployment has been disguised, with peripheral workers (notably women and older workers) being either pushed out of the labour force in recessions, or covered by temporary government subsidies or pushed into chronic "underemployment". In Japan, it is only necessary to be working for one hour in the reference week of the relevant labour force surveys to be counted as employed.

On the other hand, the more consensus and less conflict-oriented traditions in the labour market seem to have helped considerably in the transition from a muscle power to a brain power labour market.

If the lessons from Japan are not quite appropriate for Europeans, what about the "Newly Industrializing Countries" of South-East Asia and South America? Their rapid development—and, at least in South Korea, Taiwan, Singapore and Hong Kong, successful labour absorption and low unemployment—has sometimes been held out as an object lesson for Europeans concerned with high unemployment and deindustrialization. But to become "price-competitive" with the NICs Europe would have to dismantle many labour protection regulations, cut real wages and fringe benefits savagely and impose rigid controls over union activity. That route would imply severe cuts in living standards and a renunciation of labour rights obtained over generations. The success of the NICs presupposes high-income demand from Europe and the US. If they adapt to NIC wages there will be no such demand to repeat that success. Europe's competitiveness must rest with her highly-qualified manpower, and on a process of continuous innovation that can only be imitated by others with a considerable time-lag.

In sum, the specific features of labour markets in North America, Japan and the NICs do not offer models that should or even could be emulated in Western Europe.

Part VII: A Decent Standard of Living for All Citizens of Europe

The welfare state crisis

The welfare state in Europe was created on the basis of certain assumptions about the labour market and the employment structure. The basic premise was that there would be full employment and that the State had to provide income security to cover "temporary interruptions" of earning power. The second premise was that the labour force would consist predominantly of men in regular, full-time jobs, each with an economically inactive wife and dependent children. On the basis of those two premises, a social-insurance social security system could provide what the State was expected to provide, basic security from deprivation, or a subsistence level of income security. Critical to that part of the social consensus was the view that, except for a tiny minority of disadvantaged citizens, the labour market could satisfy the income needs of the population.

What has happened in the past 40 years is that the delicate balance between the social security system and the labour market has been undermined in many coun-

151

tries. Indeed, it is scarcely an exaggeration to state that the two are now in conflict.

First, there is a crisis of financing the social security system. Gradually, in the postwar era of full employment, anomalies in the original social security model were recognized and new schemes were introduced. Selective means-tested benefits were added and those left out of the mainstream of economic growth through unemployment, retirement, disability, family status, and so on were catered for. The demands for income transfers rose, but not excessively, in the era of full employment when most jobs were regular, full-time and protected.

However, with the huge growth of unemployment in the 1980s, demands and needs grew while contributions fell. And with more employed workers not in full-time work or in jobs only for short periods, social security contributions further declined. Then in some places more "flexible" payment systems led to a widespread avoidance of contributions. Although the story may differ from country to country, the essence is the same: an incipient fiscal crisis as sluggish economic growth has dampened revenues from taxes and social security contributions while claims for unemployment benefits, early retirement and subsidies for manufacturing in many countries have been rising strongly.

A demographic crisis is compounding the fiscal crisis due to mass unemployment and underemployment. In particular, the ageing of the European population is creating a growing dependency problem. In 1975 there were three people aged 20–59 for every one over age 60; in the 1990s the ratio will be less than two to one.

There has always been a social equity crisis. Along with

the growing complexity and resort to selective income support schemes, the very generality or non-discriminatory nature of social security upon which Beveridge and others so insisted has been lost. Probably a good case could be made for saying that social security has not protected the weakest groups in society. Many people have been intimidated by complex procedures. But of growing importance have been those who have not qualified for income transfers because of the nature of their labour market involvement. Workers in flexible forms of employment—temporaries, part-timers, homeworkers and other "outworkers"—have often not qualified. Various studies have shown that social security coverage is relatively weak for the self-employed, whose share of the non-agricultural labour force has grown in many countries in the past decade, particularly in Italy, Spain and the United Kingdom. The official data probably understate the extent of self-employment, including contract workers. Thus the social security system may exclude growing numbers who deserve and need to be covered.

It may be too strong to call it that, yet there is also the possibility that social security systems have created an "unemployment trap" crisis. The jobs that have been disappearing have mostly been reasonably well-paid, full-time industrial work. Those that have been growing fastest have been part-time and often lower-paid service jobs. Consequently, even though the income replacement ratio for those receiving unemployment benefits may be much less than previous (full-time) earnings, many unemployed will be discouraged from taking the available job opportunities because they would experience a decline in net income. One implication is that many male unemployed cannot sensibly take part-time job vacancies (without an income cut) while women from outside the labour force can do so. To call the resultant male unemployment "voluntary" would be absurd.

There is also an incipient moral-political crisis over social security, due partly to the fiscal and unemployment trap pressures. Attempts to check the growth of social security commitments have led to efforts to make the system more selective and "target-oriented", with a tightening up of conditionality. This has raised questions about the underlying regulatory function of social security, with somewhat arbitrary criteria for separating the deserving from the undeserving poor. In many countries, thousands of families and individuals are affected by the "poverty trap", whereby people in jobs may gain little extra or actually receive less if they work more, because of loss of benefits. Increasing selectivity increases that tendency, while as a cost-cutting measure it is unlikely to be very equitable (despite what some claim), precisely because that is not the justification of the exercise.

Finally, there is what might be called an efficiency crisis. Rather than facilitate and encourage flexible employment, the social security system makes it hard for many workers to be flexible and penalizes others who are. The difficulties of transferring pension rights is one of the most important obstacles to desirable flexibility. In general, because of qualification rules about past work, those who work intermittently are excluded in some cases or provided with minimal benefits. Social security arrangements can also discourage voluntary labour mobility where they restrict benefit receipt for those who "quit" jobs. For older workers, there is often a "retirement trap", meaning that should they wish to take a part-time job, they would lose part or all of their pension income. The "unemployment trap" also makes job experimentation impractical or potentially costly for many of the jobless, while the poverty trap penalizes those who wish to increase their work effort or skill.

Thus the problems of the labour market in Western Europe cannot be addressed without contemplating fairly radical reforms of the social security system. The two must mesh, not clash.

It will take time to bring the unemployed back to work and by that also to improve employment conditions for those in precarious employment. They must have more general income security in the meantime.

A basic income for all citizens

"A citizenship income is fast becoming feasible." (Guy Standing, at the Helsinki meeting of the Commission)

"A minimum income for everyone is a good instrument against hunger, but it keeps you poor in the long run." (Paavo Lipponen, at the Paris meeting of the Commission)

If there is no speeding-up of economic growth in the medium term, it is safe to predict that income inequality will worsen, and that payment systems will continue to become more flexible, involving greater use of bonuses, fringe benefits, share options, profit-related pay and so on for core workers and management. But for a growing number of people, precarious forms of employment will be the usual experience.

Illegal or clandestine economic activity seems to be

growing in many European countries. The important point is that the incentives and opportunities for such informal employment are increasing.

For many, the future would seem bleak. But a crisis in the original Greek sense means not only a failure but an opportunity. To turn a potential disaster into the basis for a new social consensus, policies are needed that facilitate economic growth, encourage efficient and flexible use of labour and above all provide income security. As many people as possible should be enabled to do useful work, to be creative and to contribute to social as well as personal welfare.

Some members of the Commission were of the opinion that it would be very hard for governments to improve the labour market situation sufficiently. They therefore urged that income security, a basic income provided as a right of citizenship, should be placed on the political agenda. The principle is that all or most benefits (including indirect benefits handed out in the form of tax reliefs) should be replaced by a single transfer income (given as a tax credit to income earners, or as a cash payment to others), with supplements to cover specific needs, such as disability, that imply a higher cost of living for particular individuals. The citizenship income would be paid to all individuals, regardless of age (though lower for children below the age of 16), sex, marital status, and duration of past work or tax-paying. All earned income above the citizenship income would be taxable, with a comprehensive income tax replacing the existing income tax and social security contributions.

A citizenship income would facilitate more flexible forms of employment, making it easier for people to combine part-time work with other activities. It would encourage "work-sharing", for which there seems to be a widespread desire. By removing the unemployment trap it would enable some unemployed men to take part-time employment. By reducing the risk of penury in the event of failure, it would encourage self-employment.

It would help break down the sexual division of labour, and achieve more sexual equity in the labour market, by improving women's bargaining position (notably those trapped in low-wage, insecure jobs) and by encouraging men to take part-time jobs, so allowing them to take a greater share of child care and domestic forms of work.

It would help remove the arbitrary and inflexible notion of retirement age, while enabling older workers to avoid the unfair penalization of earnings rules that in some countries determines receipt of state pensions. It would also encourage worklife interruptions to learn new skills. Ways need to be found to enable the rapidly growing number of older workers to continue to use their abilities and experience for the benefit of themselves and their communities.

By providing basic income security as a right of citizenship, it would reduce the stigma of unemployment while dispensing with the current situation in which many receive benefits only if they remain idle.

Thus a citizenship income guarantee system would facilitate labour flexibility and would help to prevent "workfare" and "targeting" (tightening the rules for eligibility to state benefits). Finally, a universal income scheme would reduce the dependence of the poor and the unemployed on a welfare system that in effect regulates, monitors and stigmatizes them.

The main criticisms of a citizenship income scheme,

brought forward by some other members of the Commission, are threefold:

— it would involve explicit acceptance of the inability of the State to provide jobs for all;
— it would be very costly, in many countries involving a substantial increase in the total burden of taxation; and
— it would act as a disincentive to people to take on necessary low-productivity jobs.

A citizenship income scheme nevertheless merits serious consideration by governments. Even it is not a feasible solution for today's problems, it may be a solution for tomorrow.

What is advocated in this report is the opportunity for all who wish it to find satisfying employment. For those without such employment, income security must be guaranteed one way or the other. The introduction of a minimum income in France is a step in the right direction.

Part VIII: Summary

"Most of the keys to full employment are problems of courage, either intellectual or political courage." (Michel Rocard, at the constituent meeting of the Commission in Vienna)

Twenty million Europeans—more than 11 per cent of the labour force—are out of work and on present trends mass unemployment looks set to persist well into the 1990s. Years of sluggish economic growth, even the stronger growth registered in 1988, have failed to make inroads into the jobless total. It is all too possible that another recession, whenever that comes, could drive up unemployment once again and, swell the numbers in precarious low-paid jobs.

The fact that unemployment is so unevenly spread over areas, age and skill groups has made it difficult to fashion policies commanding widespread support for strong positive action to cut the dole queues. Governments have also been reluctant to tackle unemployment directly because of fears of inflation and budget deficits.

All this has contributed to a mood of political defeatism and social apathy in the face of persistently high levels of joblessness. This report tries to point the way towards a new strategy designed to reduce the unemploy-

159

ment rate to around 5 per cent by the mid-1990s—the level prevailing in the late 1970s.

We are proposing a concerted effort by the European economies to boost the rate of economic growth from the $2\frac{1}{2}$ per cent a year currently projected to an employment-generating 3.5 per cent or more. We are suggesting a set of measures that can stimulate long-run economic developments and, at the same time, "twist" the nature of economic growth in such a way as to minimize environmental damage and maximize the generation of high-quality jobs, including jobs for those largely bypassed by market forces such as the long-term unemployed.

It is a strategy which has a broader aim: the enhancement of the quality of life for all Europe's citizens, through opportunities for satisfying employment, a better environment and cultural enrichment. It is based on a belief that the path to prosperity lies not in providing low-wage, low-skill jobs but in upgrading and exploiting to the full Europe's stock of skilled and educated labour.

Unemployment is enormously costly, to the individual affected and his family, to society and to the economy. The repercussions of mass joblessness are felt by everyone—in a more divided society in which many people are unable to share the full benefits of citizenship, in the growth of poverty, in poorer job and career prospects for new generations of workers, and in political destabilization. The costs of unemployment, taken together, may outweigh the expense to the community of creating jobs. In Sweden, one of the richest countries in Europe where the jobless rate is around 2 per cent, the saying goes that the country is not rich enough to afford the luxury of unemployment.

We do not share the view sometimes expressed that high unemployment is simply a problem of rigid labour markets, excessive real labour costs and over-generous unemployment benefits. The Commission rejects the route to cutting unemployment based solely on making labour markets more flexible. That could mean higher numbers of "working poor", as has happened in the United States. In circumstances where Europe as a whole has been running a surplus in the balance of payments, a beggar-thy-neighbour policy of cutting real wages to become more competitive internationally would not only be self-defeating but would tend to aggravate existing global imbalances.

Towards a new social consensus

We argue for a co-ordinated programme of European expansion, which will ensure that risks for the balance of payments and government indebtedness are minimized. The risk of inflation should be mitigated by incomes policy checking inflationary wage demands, by commodity price stabilization and by labour market policy reducing wage drift.

The need for European economic co-operation is reinforced by the drive within the 12-member European Community towards a barrier-free internal market by the end of 1992. A study prepared for the European Commission has estimated that this could create between 2 and 5 million jobs. But the Commission has itself acknowledged that the full benefits of market integration will be reaped only with fast economic growth, and has proposed a co-operative growth strategy which we see as an essential minimum, but to which governments have only paid lip-service.

More rapid economic expansion is necessary but not sufficient to make a substantial dent in unemployment. Unspecified expansion, for instance through lower taxes, risks increasing inflation without reducing unemployment. The main reason for this is the enormous disparity in unemployment betwen regions and skill groups. There is a danger that regional disparities will widen in the absence of special measures to attract investment and jobs to depressed areas and to increase geographical mobility. The long-term unemployed, the low-skilled, young people with little experience of permanent employment, are all likely to be left behind if market forces are left to their own devices.

We are therefore advocating a strategy that "twists" the nature of economic growth in ways that will provide job opportunities for the most disadvantaged groups, at the same time as promoting skilled employment and protecting the environment.

Our programme focuses on investment-led expansion, based on a wide range of projects capable of creating many millions of jobs and improving the quality of life. This would be backed up by labour market policies designed to reduce obstacles to growth and aid vulnerable groups in the labour force, notably the young and the long-term unemployed through training, retraining and "education through life". Shorter and more flexible working hours should increase the employment effects of an expansionary programme. In addition, the State must do more to ensure income security.

A six-point programme for Europe

Our Commission's view is that the prevailing microeconomic and market-oriented strategies may help somewhat, but will by no means be sufficient to cut unemployment. We therefore need some kind of long-term macroeconomic planning to fight unemployment through tackling the major problems of our time.

We are proposing a six-point programme for economic expansion in Europe that is mainly concerned with the improvement of the environment and the much neglected physical, intellectual and cultural infrastructure in Europe.

1. Environmental protection

Concern for the environment in any future growth strategy is essential to ensure that growth is sustainable and contributes to the quality of life, and to blunt antipathy to expansion seen in a number of Western European countries.

Higher growth rates are necessary to generate more resources to remedy environmental damage and prevent future deterioration. But it requires immediate political action to use these resources for environmental protection. Governments increasingly have become aware of the positive employment effects of environmental policies. Environmental protection is not a jobkiller, but a jobmaker. The positive net employment effects of environmental protection will be the higher, the more active environmental policies are.

The share of spending on environmental protection in

GDP and employment has to be at least doubled to solve just the ecological problems of the day. Research and development directed towards finding less polluting and damaging production and consumption methods is also urgently needed.

If Europe—both East and West—wants to remain a place fit to live in for generations to come, a new approach to environmental protection is essential immediately. Otherwise accumulated damage could become irreparable.

Technical and financial co-operation between East and West in Europe is vital, since pollution control does not respect national frontiers. Parts of the large credits now granted to the Eastern countries should be earmarked for pollution control.

Environmental projects may be on a mammoth or small scale, involving private and public investment, and financed, for example, through users' fees, taxes on energy and higher prices for "clean" products. The main impetus should come from stricter national regulations that enforce private investment to save our environment. Stricter international regulations on environmental standards are also needed to prevent "environmental dumping" and to secure the efficacy of anti-pollution efforts.

2. Infrastructure

Cuts in public spending have resulted in a large backlog need for infrastructure investment. In many European countries, infrastructure investment is now half of what it had been in the early 1970s. Urgent priorities vary considerably between countries and regions but include efficient telecommunications networks, urban and village renewal, housing for the young, the old and migrant labour, high-speed rail connections and transnational transport links.

The European governments must together develop the infrastructure investment necessary to reap the fruits of their big endeavour to create a single market by 1992. Small changes in the infrastructure tend to result in large changes in the economic structure.

Such an increase in infrastructure investment will not only satisfy urgent needs, but also stimulate private investment that has been restrained during the 1980s. Immediate results from this policy will be evident for all citizens.

The necessary finance should come from a better collaboration between the public and the private sectors. Due to fiscal constraints, the financing of such projects must shift from the public to the private sector. This is a crucial difference to the past. In the words of one Commission member: "As much private finance as possible, as much public finance as necessary." Public tasks need not be solely public expenditures, as the project for the Channel tunnel demonstrates. We strongly support the proposals of the Round Table of European Industrialists, the Confederation of Nordic and German Trade Unions and the German Bundesanstalt für Arbeit on boosting infrastructure investment.

3. Technology and innovation

Europe's technological potential must be strengthened in order to maintain competitiveness as well as to sustain high living standards and the quality of life. Europe needs to develop an integrated technology and innovation policy, concentrated on research and more especially development, to help facilitate industrial adjustment. So far, common efforts have been ridiculously small, compared with the United States and Japan. Such a policy would do more in the long run to create decent new jobs than a short-sighted policy of preserving at high cost existing jobs in uncompetitive industries.

There has been an impressive resurgence of more flexible and specialized small enterprises. Considering the concentration process in Europe, reinforced by the completion of the single market, stimulus is required in particular for small and medium sized firms that cannot carry out the necessary research and development on their own.

4. Culture and education

Central and local governments should endeavour to expand cultural activities to stimulate open-mindedness, experimentation and imagination, and to satisfy unmet cultural and educational needs. There is a close relationship between technology, culture and education. The qualities encouraged by culture are also those required for technological innovation. Education provides the basic foundation for research and development and for the appreciation of culture.

In many European countries educational and cultural needs are not being fully satisfied—for example, obsolete and deficient school-systems, adult education and most cultural needs outside the cities—while increasing numbers of well-educated people are jobless or underemployed.

The educational system must be made more flexible at all levels to be able to adapt both curricula and learning methods to present and future needs. It should also concentrate more on inventiveness and problem solving. Special care must be taken to ensure that the disadvantaged to stay in touch with the training system, preventing them from dropping out early and becoming "untrainable" for qualified jobs.

Regional decentralization of cultural activities is required to satisfy unmet cultural needs outside the cities.

We need a better co-operation between the private and the public sectors to raise funds for cultural and educational activities that are always labour- and skill-intensive.

Generally speaking, business will tend to sponsor traditional, widely appreciated culture (for publicity reasons); the public sector will have to finance experimentation in other fields.

5. Information services

Intermediate services to other producers (such as software, databanks and consulting) are among the fastest growing sectors in the West. An efficient telecommunications network is a precondition for the development of these new information and communications services, just as roads and railways were for traditional industries. There is a particular lack of this infrastructure in the south of Europe.

Information services give young entrepreneurs wide scope to start new businesses. This should be encouraged, for instance, by removing bureaucratic obstacles to trade.

6. East-West and North-South trade relations

Improved trade relations, economic co-operation and, for the poorest developing countries, a big expansion of official aid, would be in the interests of both sides of the East-West, North-South divide.

Glasnost and *perestroika* make co-operation with Eastern European countries more feasible than before, while cross-border environmental problems make it more vital than ever.

An improvement of East-West and North-South trade relations would provide a powerful impetus for new investment and employment in Europe.

Many projects of our six-point programme are or can be on a small scale, well-suited for small business. To finance them we need organizational innovation to create new forms of co-operation between the private and the public sector, as well as lower interest rates.

However, it is worth stressing that the costs of most of the projects are scarcely higher, if at all, than the direct and indirect costs of unemployment. Expansionary policies will barely increase budget and balance of payment deficits if European countries act together.

As an adjunct to existing financing mechanisms for cross-national projects there is a good case for exploring the establishment of a European Bank for Infrastructure which could be funded by governments and the private sector.

The restrictive policies, which brought about high

unemployment in Europe were motivated by the inflationary pressure that emerged after the two oil price shocks and this problem has not been definitely solved. The new growth policy thus has to be more inflation-resistant. Much of the inflation was initially caused by rising commodity prices. Governments in Western Europe should, therefore, initiate and foster world-wide co-operation to establish more efficient commodity production and price stabilization schemes. Government and labour market organizations should also develop incomes policies to bridle nominal wage increases to avoid wage-push monopolistic profits. An efficient labour market policy should be adopted in all countries to dampen wage drift at higher levels of employment and to reduce training costs for enterprises which increase their workforce.

The regional dimension

Unemployment in Europe shows wide regional disparities. In Germany, for example, jobless rates vary from 11 to 13 per cent in the northern regions dominated by now-declining industries such as shipyards and steel, to virtually full employment in the south which has enjoyed an economic revival based on high-tech and service industries. In Britain and some other countries, regional disparities in unemployment rates are increasing as market-led economic growth fails to make inroads into long-term unemployment in depressed areas.

The reduction of unemployment in these areas needs to be given priority. Market-oriented strategies and national macroeconomic policies (tax cuts and reform, interest rate cuts and so on) will not be sufficient on their own.

The projects we propose should, wherever feasible, be focused on disadvantaged regions. Where the regions concerned cannot afford high expenditure for environmental protection, urban renewal, education and culture, industrial parks and the like—all necessary to attract new firms and highly qualified employees—central government should provide financial aid. However, help from government will not be enough without initiatives at the local level which will be self-sustaining.

Making such regions more attractive to investors would create new jobs where they are most urgently needed and open the door for a revival of the local economy.

Twisting the nature of growth

Twisting the nature of growth is a long-run strategy to make use of Europe's greatest potential competitive strength—the high skills of its population.

All our proposals are addressed to some of the major economic and social concerns of the day, but all too are designed to help improve the quality of employment. This is most evident with new jobs in research, development, culture and education, though urban renewal, telecommunications and information services also provide many skilled jobs. Environmental projects not only "twist" the nature of growth towards a better environment but may raise the skill content of growth, since pollution control and energy saving need considerable research into new technologies and much more training and retraining.

In our view, it is not an appropriate long-run strategy to cut European wages and social standards in order to create low-wage jobs in the low-productivity service sector or to prevent low-wage industries from shrinking. Nor should governments aim to create low-skill jobs on the grounds that unemployment among the unskilled is particularly high. Given the long-run transition from "muscle-power" to "brain-power" the need is to train people in the right skills for the future. A forward-looking strategy, not a defensive one, is required. More high-quality jobs would enable the skills of the labour force to be upgraded, as happened in the early postwar decades. Many employees will move into higher-skill categories, assisted by retraining measures and adult education, and so set jobs free for the less-skilled unemployed.

Labour market policies

To reinforce the strategy of investment-led expansion, an active manpower policy will be needed to smooth structural changes, overcome obstacles to growth and help prevent the resurgence of inflation. Labour market policies should also be geared to stimulating permanent employment for those who would otherwise find themselves bypassed by increased job opportunities.

To make a substantial reduction in unemployment possible without inflationary pressure, it will be necessary to improve the functioning of the labour market. An efficient labour exchange is indispensable to match suitable jobs and applicants.

The large regional and skill-specific disparities in unemployment must be tackled directly through labour market policies. Retraining programmes and financial incentives for the start-up of firms are preferable to preserving unprofitable jobs in declining industries.

A training or work guarantee for the long-term unemployed has been introduced in some Scandinavian countries and proposed elsewhere. People who have been unemployed for more than a year have the right to a job or a retraining course. Such guarantees are useful in preventing long-term unemployed and other disadvantaged groups from losing contact with the labour market.

One important labour market issue is the reduction of working time. Shorter working hours cannot increase the amount of work available but to some extent they can distribute it more evenly and so generate more jobs with any given expansion. The cost will normally be a smaller increase in real wages—either through more moderate wage claims or through higher prices—for those already employed. For employers extra costs may be offset by reduced claims for wages and fringe benefits.

Shorter working hours would be best combined with greater flexibility of working time to improve utilization of plant and equipment, to reduce bottlenecks of skilled workers and ensure better availability of public and private services. Greater working time flexibility should include more flexible opening hours, more scope for voluntary part-time work (especially for married women) and, of increasing importance, more flexible retirement. There will be positive medium-term employment effects of shorter and more flexible working hours, but their effects on unemployment should not be overestimated.

In any case, it will take a number of years to reduce unemployment in Europe to acceptable levels. Even at the end of this period, there will be several million unemployed left. We must therefore guarantee that all have means of subsistence. A minimum standard of income security is needed for those who cannot claim unemployment benefits and for the "working poor" who hold insecure low-paid jobs as well as for those on the dole. Increasing numbers of people are now falling through the insurance net because they cannot meet qualifying conditions or their entitlement period for benefit has run out.

Conclusion

The message of this report is a positive one—much can be done to tackle unemployment in Europe. It requires a co-operative European effort to boost growth, complemented by measures that "twist" growth towards environmental protection and promoting high-skill jobs and thus enhance the quality of life. We believe our proposed programme is timely: constraints to growth are less burdensome than for many years and the programme meshes well with European Community moves to a barrier-free internal market in 1992. Further, after a decade of unnecessarily high unemployment, people, including practical politicians, are surely ready to accept that new remedies should be tried. The unemployed themselves, and those on the margins of productive society, deserve better than they have received over the last ten years.

For the long-term unemployed and other vulnerable groups there is little time to lose if they are to be given hope of re-integration into the labour market and thus into the mainstream of national life. For society as a whole, mass unemployment is a corrosive influence in the community and a costly drain on the economy. In the very long run it may pose a real threat to democracy itself. After world peace, we see no greater priority.

Appendix: The Commission and Its Work

The Commission on Employment Issues in Europe is an independent body consisting of experts, industrialists, trade union officials and politicians.

Eight meetings were held over $2\frac{1}{2}$ years, and about 25 papers were submitted to the Commission. The report of the Commission is based on these papers and the oral contributions of the participants. The near-100 participants of the meetings do not necessarily endorse the entire report for which Ewald Walterskirchen and Clas-Erik Odhner were primarily responsible. The composition of the Commission partly changed from meeting to meeting. Thus, a large number of people were able to contribute.

The Commission would like to thank the governments of Finland, Sweden, Austria, Norway and Luxemburg for their financial contributions. The Commission wishes also to thank the organizers of the meetings: Fritz Klocker and his co-workers, Miguel Nigorra, David Lea, Paavo Lipponen and Georg Lennkh.

Meetings of the Commission

Vienna: 16 September 1986
Vienna: 5 and 6 December 1986

Vienna: 3 and 4 April 1987
Palma: 19 and 20 June 1987
Vienna: 16 and 17 October 1987
London: 28 to 30 January 1988
Helsinki: 22 and 23 April 1988
Paris: 9 and 10 January 1989

The Commission

President
Bruno KREISKY
Former Federal Chancellor of Austria

Scientific Coordination
Ewald WALTERSKIRCHEN
Austrian Institute for Economic Research

Administration
Friedrich KLOCKER
Secretary of the Austrian Socialist Party

Auditor
Karl VAK
Managing Director of Zentralsparkasse and Kommer-
zialbank, Austria

Secretariat
Susanna BOKOR
Address: Schwarzenbergplatz 16, A-1011 Vienna, Aus-
tria

Participants
Awn AL-ANI, UNICEF, Jordan

Karl S. ALTHALER, Institute for Advanced Studies, Austria

Erich ANDRLIK, Director of the Vienna Institute for Development, Austria

Raymond BARRE, Former Prime Minister, France

Christian BELIERES, FO, France

Amit BHADURI, Professor of Economics, New Delhi, India

Kurt Hans BIEDENKOPF, Member of a provincial diet, Professor, Germany

Francis BLANCHARD, Director General, International Labor Office, Geneva, Switzerland

Ferdinando BORLETTI, Industrialist, Chairman "24 Ore", Italy

Roger BRIESCH, International Secretary, CFDT, France

Karl-Heinz BRODERSEN, Entrepreneur, President of Board of Technocell AG, Germany

Horst BRUM, Trade Union for Public Services and Transport, Germany

Willem BUITER, Professor of Economics at the London School of Economics, Great Britain

Peter COLDRICK, Confederal Secretary, European Trade Union Confederation, Brussels, Belgium

Jose M. ESCONDRILLAS, President of Union Explosivos Riotinto, Madrid, Spain

John EVANS, General Secretary of TUAC (Trade Union Advisory Committee to the OECD), Paris, France

Paul FABRA, Journalist, *Le Monde*, France

Hans FALSTRÖM, expert for developing countries, Sweden

Georg FISCHER, coordinator of labour market

research, Ministry of Labour and Social Affairs, Austria

John Kenneth GALBRAITH, Professor at Harvard University, United States

Michel GASPARD, Commissariat General du Plan, France

Geoffrey GOODMAN, Journalist, Great Britain

Manuel GUASCH, President of FASA-RENAULT, Madrid, Spain

Mathias HINTERSCHEID, General Secretary of the European Trade Union Confederation, Brussels, Belgium

Claus HOFMANN, consultant, Commission of the European Communities, Brussels, Belgium

Hilmar HOFFMANN, expert on cultural issues, politician, Germany

Richard HOGGART, Professor at Goldsmith College, Great Britain

Mikael INGBERG, Research Institute on the Finnish Economy, Helsinki, Finland

Marie JAHODA, Professor of Social Psychology, Sussex, Great Britain

Kari KAIRAMO, Chairman of NOKIA, Finland (died in December 1988)

Jean KASPAR, General Secretary, CFDT, France

Pekka KORPINEN, Director of the Labour Institute for Economic Research, Helsinki, Finland

Dieter KRAMER, expert on cultural issues, Federal Republic of Germany

Hans-Jürgen KRUPP, Finanzstadtrat in Hamburg, Professor of Economics, Germany

Jermu LAINE, General Director of Finnish Customs, former Minister, Finland

David LEA, Assistant General Secretary, Trades Union Congress, Great Britain

Alain LEBAUBE, Journalist, *Le Monde*, France

Georg LENNKH, Austrian Ambassador to OECD, Paris, France

Paavo LIPPONEN, Director of the Finnish Institute of International Affairs, Helsinki, Finland

Egon MATZNER, Director of the Wissenschaftszentrum Berlin, Professor of Economics, Germany

Nicholas MERCURO, Professor of Environmental Economics, New Orleans, United States

Alistair MORTON, Co-Chairman of Eurotunnel, Great Britain

Karl-Heinz NACHTNEBEL, International Secretary of the Austrian Trade Union Confederation

Miguel NIGORRA, President of Banco Credito Balear, Mallorca

Clas-Erik ODHNER, Former chief economist of the Swedish Trade Union Confederation (LO)

John PALMER, Journalist, *The Guardian*, London

Gunter A. PAULI, General Secretary of the European Service Industries Forum, Belgium

Jukka PEKKARINEN, Deputy Director of the Labour Institute for Economic Research, Helsinki, Finland

Bjorn PETTERSSON, Former Deputy General Secretary of the European Trade Union Confederation, Sweden

Edgar PLAN, Director of the Kredietbank, Brussels, Belgium

Robert PONTILLON, Senator, President Franco-British Council, Paris, France

Stephen POTTER, Director, Economic Affairs, OECD, Paris, France

Robert H. PRY, Director of IIASA, Laxenburg, Austria

Stephen K. PURSEY, International Confederation of Free Trade Unions, Belgium

Gosta REHN, Professor, former Director of the OECD Manpower and Social Affairs Committee, Sweden

Jose Ramon Alavarez RENDUELES, Professor, Banco Zaragozano, Madrid, Spain

Michel ROCARD, Prime Minister of France

Heinz RUHNAU, President of Deutsche Lufthansa AG, former Under-Secretary of State, Germany

Fritz W. SCHARPF, Director of the Max-Planck-Institut für Gesellschaftsforschung, Professor, Germany

Michele SALVATI, Professor of Economics, Milan, Italy

Gunter SCHMID, labour market expert, Wissenschaftszentrum Berlin, Germany

Ludwig SCHUBERT, Director, Commission of the European Communities, Brussels, Belgium

Conrad SEIDL, Journalist, *Kurier*, Austria

Guy STANDING, coordinator of labour market research, Employment Department, International Labour Office, Geneva, Switzerland

Günther STEINBACH, Sektionsleiter, Ministry of Labour and Social Affairs, Austria

Alfred STROER, Director, Bank für Arbeit und Wirtschaft, former Leading Secretary of the Austrian Trade Union Confederation

Friedrich SVIHALEK, General Secretary of the youth section of trade unions, Austria

Herbert TIEBER, Member of Parliament, Austria

Jacques TROESCH, consultant, France

Anneli VALPOLA, Vice-President of WÄRTSILA, Helsinki, Finland

Lucien VARDA, L'Oréal, France

Jose Maria VICZAINO, Manager, San Sebastian, Spain

Pierre VINDE, Deputy Secretary General, OECD, Paris, France

Heinz VOGLER, President of the Austrian Chamber of Labour

Michael WAGNER, Director of the Institute for Economic and Social Research, Austria

Helen WALLACE, Royal Institute of Economic Affairs, London, Great Britain

Lord WEDDERBURN, Professor of Law at the London School of Economics, Great Britain

Frances WILLIAMS, Journalist, Geneva, Switzerland

Monika WULF-MATHIES, President of the Trade Union for Public Services and Transport, Germany

David YOUNG, Economist Intelligence Unit, London, Great Britain

Karl Georg ZINN, Professor of Economics, Aachen, Germany

References

1. OECD Economic Surveys: *United Kingdom* (Paris, January 1985), p.32.
2. Robert J. Flanagan, Labour Market Behaviour and European Economic Growth, manuscript, September 1986.
3. *Full Employment and Growth as the Social and Economic Goal.* A Joint Statement by BIAC and TUAC, the employer and trade union advisory committees to the OECD, Paris 1986.
4. P. Lazarsfeld, M. Jahoda and E. Zeisel, *The unemployed in Marienthal, Suhrkamp*, 1979 (new edition).
5. R.Z. Lawrence and C.W. Schultze, *Barriers to European Growth*, Brookings Institution, Washington, 1987.
6. Commission of the European Communities: "Annual Economic Report 1988–89", *European Economy*, November 1988.
7. Brundtland Commission report: *Our Common Future*, 1987.
8. Paolo Cecchini, *Europe 1992. The Advantage of the Internal Market*, 1988.
9. Beretta Report: *Social Aspects of the Internal Market*, Brussels, 1987.
10. OECD: *Employment Outlook*, Paris, 1986.
11. OECD: *A Medium-Term Strategy for Employment and Manpower Policies*, Paris, 1978.
12. For example, the Nordic and German unions study: *It Pays to Co-operate*, 1983.
13. Round Table of European Industrialists: *Promotion and Financing of Great Infrastructure Projects in Europe*, February 1986.

14. Commission of the European Communities: *European Economy* No.30, November 1986, p.108.
15. Nordic and German Unions, *Challenge for Europe*, 1986.
16. *The European Community and the Environment*, No.3, 1987.
17. SPD: *Employment and Environment*, 1985.
18. M. Piore and Ch. Sabel, *The Second Industrial Divide*, New York, 1984, p.19.
19. Hilmar Hoffman, *Culture for Tomorrow*, 1985.
20. Misha Glenny, "Living in a Socialist Smog", *New Scientist*, 24 September 1987, p.41.
21. Brandt Commission report: *North–South: A Programme for Survival*, 1980, p.20.
22. *Financial Times*, 29 March 1988.
23. UNIDO: 1986 Report, p.97.
24. *It Pays to Co-operate*, op. cit.
25. Cecchini Report, op. cit.; Tommaso Padoa-Schioppa, *Efficiency, Stability and Equity*, Oxford, 1987.
26. Richard Layard, *How to Beat Unemployment*, Oxford, 1986.
27. Brookings Institution, op. cit.
28. Physician Task Force on Hunger in America, Harvard School of Public Health, *Hunger Reaches Blue-Collar America*, 1987.
29. Martin Weitzman, *The Share Economy*, Harvard, 1984.

Dr Bruno Kreisky was born in 1911, and from an early age was involved in the emerging Austrian Social Democratic movement. After being arrested by the Gestapo on several occasions during the 1930s, he was forced into exile in Sweden throughout the Second World War, where he worked as an economic consultant and journalist. On his return to Austria in May 1946, he joined the Austrian foreign service, and, for the next decade, worked for the Federal Chancellery, being appointed Minister of State for the Foreign Affairs Section in 1953.

In 1956, he was elected to the Austrian parliament and embarked upon a political career which has been both long and illustrious. His experience in foreign affairs contributed to his appointment as Foreign Minister three years later. By 1967, Kreisky was Chairman of the Austrian Socialist Party, and, in April 1970, was sworn in as Chancellor of Austria. For the next 13 years, Kreisky not only dominated Austrian politics, but also continued his work for improved international relations, taking part in several fact-finding missions to the Middle East in his capacity as a Vice-President of the Socialist International, and playing a leading role in international diplomatic developments. His work in this area was recognised in 1984 when he was awarded the Jawarharlal Nehru Award for promoting international understanding. He continues to play an active role in European politics and the promotion of world preace.